career
conversations

career
conversations

How to get
the best
from your
talent pool

Greg Smith

WILEY

First published in 2019 by John Wiley & Sons Australia, Ltd
42 McDougall St, Milton Qld 4064

Office also in Melbourne

Typeset in 11/15 pt ITC Berkeley Oldstyle Std

© John Wiley & Sons Australia, Ltd 2019

ISBN: 9780730371991

The moral rights of the author have been asserted

 A catalogue record for this
book is available from the
National Library of Australia

Cover design by Wiley

Cover image: © Mark Heider / Shutterstock

Internal image: © cajoer/iStockphoto

10 9 8 7 6 5 4 3 2 1

Disclaimer
The material in this publication is of the nature of general comment only, and does not represent professional advice. It is not intended to provide specific guidance for particular circumstances and it should not be relied on as the basis for any decision to take action or not take action on any matter which it covers. Readers should obtain professional advice where appropriate, before making any such decision. To the maximum extent permitted by law, the author and publisher disclaim all responsibility and liability to any person, arising directly or indirectly from any person taking or not taking action based on the information in this publication.

Contents

To my wife, Sue, for her inspiration, encouragement and support while I wrote this book and followed my crazy dreams.

About the author

Greg Smith is an expert in the fields of career development, talent management and organisational leadership. He has more than 20 years' experience as a coach, mentor and consultant, and has led local and international commercial and consulting businesses in numerous senior executive roles. He holds a Master of Career Development and is a Certified Practising Marketer (CPM).

A career highlight was co-founding deliberatepractice, a highly successful and specialised HR consulting firm, which he headed up as managing partner and chief executive.

Greg's career focus today is helping aspiring, emerging and experienced leaders to develop their knowledge skills in guiding the careers of the people they lead and to build this capacity into their everyday leadership skill set. His inspiration for writing this book was to share the secrets of holding effective career conversations that he has learned over a long and varied leadership career.

Preface

This book was written for organisational leaders at all levels. I have deliberately avoided writing a conventional 'careers book'. I'll admit, when I first contemplated writing a book in the careers field, I thought it would lean towards self-help advice for people facing career transition. However, after coaching literally hundreds of executives and seeing firsthand the positive difference career development makes to their overall leadership effectiveness, I was drawn towards a different focus. I decided to write this guide for leaders seeking to develop their skills in holding career conversations and to build this capability into their *everyday* leadership skill kit.

More specifically, I wanted to share with you, as leaders, the secrets of holding effective career conversations I have discovered through my experience as a leader and careers and coaching expert, as well as from the top researchers and practitioners in these fields. My goal was to provide an easy-to-read and practical guide to leading better, fear-free career conversations in the pursuit of career satisfaction.

Grounded in theoretical and applied aspects of contemporary career management, my approach is underpinned by the research showing career satisfaction to be a key driver of personal and business success through superior talent management and strong leadership capability.

Career Conversations synthesises my accumulated experience in leading organisations at the chief executive level with my professional and academic experience in marketing, careers leadership, education and development over the past 30 years. I use real-world career stories throughout the book to illustrate the models and techniques recommended, although I have changed the names and industries for privacy.

I owe much of my learning to a number of colleagues, professionals, trusted advisers and friends whom I have had the great fortune to work with throughout my career. I have drawn on their invaluable experience, wisdom and insights in these pages.

This book offers leaders an accessible, easily navigable road map with which to guide their employees through their careers and towards achievement of their own career satisfaction. Most importantly, it works!

Introduction

Careers facilitate social engagement and play an important role in creating and defining meaning in our lives. Our careers help to shape our work and personal lives.

I believe everyone has a right to career satisfaction, which is a fundamental source of energy, creativity and capability. For many, however, career satisfaction can be as elusive as self-esteem. That said, when career harmony does exist, problems of the greatest complexity seem to be solved more quickly and easily. The positive impact on our lives is palpable and exciting. The payoff of better career conversations can therefore be remarkable.

In my experience, many leaders are fearful of confronting a lack of career satisfaction and its consequences, preferring to ignore the realities that surround them. Despite all that has been written and said about employees as 'free agents', I continue to be amazed at just how many leaders still feel ill equipped and reluctant to have meaningful career conversations with their employees. The implications of employee–organisational relationships on individual career development and the co-dependencies at play cannot be understated.

Employees got the message loud and clear long ago that it was up to them to manage their own careers, but many don't know how to navigate their career pathways and receive little help from their manager or employer. I have found that many leaders lack career management and coaching skills to assist them; indeed, quite a few are fearful of the most basic career discussions. This has resulted in their delegating this aspect of their leadership responsibility to Human Resources or outsourcing it entirely to an external career coach. No matter how capably handled, neither option is likely to be as valuable in helping employees with their career development as if you, their leader, delivered it!

Some leaders believe discussing career aspirations may unsettle their employees or, worse, drive them to unrealistic career aspirations or demands. Either way, it seems many fear that beginning a career conversation risks opening up a discussion they would rather not have. This could not be further from what's actually needed.

It might surprise leaders imbued with these views to know that their employees routinely think about their career much of the time, whether asked about it or not. Leaders need to be acutely attuned all the time to their employee's state of mind with regard to their career and relationship with the organisation. They should be agile and committed in how, when and where they engage with their employees, especially when it comes to their careers. This requires leaders to build this commitment and flexibility into their leadership routine. I discuss the importance of agility with regard to leadership and career conversations in chapter 1.

Some leaders can feel frustrated (even angry) when under siege from competitors that ruthlessly and relentlessly attempt (in many cases successfully) to lure away their top talent. You can be 100 per cent certain that your competitors are approaching your top talent right now to 'feel them out'. They may use talent scout specialists as well as sophisticated research techniques and social media campaigns designed to encourage employees to question their job satisfaction and whether their needs and aspirations are being met by their current employer. Such competitor tactics can be a powerful source of employee career destabilisation.

Technology has facilitated these covert operations by making them much simpler and more cost effective to implement. I like to think of it as your competitor's 'silent army' working systematically to steal your top talent and provoke unwelcome resignations, often at the worst time!

As a leader, you have limited power to defend against competitors' approaches to your employees, which are largely out of your control. Even if you could retaliate, I strongly advise against it to avoid harming the trust between you and your employee.

The best way to counter such competitor attacks is by positively investing in your relationships with employees, taking an active, dynamic and ongoing interest in their career development, beginning with one-to-one career conversations. In my experience, when this is done well, employees will often feel more comfortable, less defensive and more likely to disclose competitor approaches without awkward probing questions from you. Make sure you always keep in mind that if you are not taking care of your best employees you can be sure your competitors will. Trust me when I say this is your best defence against unwanted competitor attacks on your employees.

Looking at retention of talent more broadly, underlying the explicit career forces at work are the implicit, subtle stimuli that can generate career doubts. These can have their roots in the recruitment process, when exaggerated promises are made by the hiring manager in the excitement of pre-employment interviews—promises that then fail to materialise. Inflated promises or representations, explicit or implied, are remembered and evaluated by employees when they come to work every day. The organisation's failure to measure up to its promises tests organisational trust and sows career doubts.

Telltale signs of this problem take many forms. For example, employees may become overly critical of the organisation and start to complain about their salary or other financial conditions. Or they may spend time revising their résumé, searching online job boards and posting on social networking sites coded or open messages that they're on the market. These explicit or implicit signals of career dissatisfaction are a window to the true state of career satisfaction that employees may, or may not, be willing to share with their leader. They can result in a 'silent' disconnection from their leader or the organisation that may be fully recognised only when an employee hands in their notice, when it's usually too late to recover the employment relationship.

Summing up

This book provides practical techniques and essential tools you'll need as a leader to get on the front foot in facilitating rewarding career discussions. The rest is up to you and practice. The more conversations you have with them, the better you will become in helping your employees realise their career aspirations. Think of it this way: you have nothing to lose (except your employees!) and everything to gain by retaining them. In an ever more competitive employment market of 'free agents' and portfolio careers, these are powerful tools for driving business success.

Chapter 1
The case for proactive career development

'It is never too late to be what you might have been.'
George Eliot

The impact on labour markets of demographic changes, together with emerging skill shortages and the rise of talent management initiatives, has prompted organisations to consider innovative attraction and retention strategies. In recent times succession management has become an organisational priority. Indeed, it is now high on the agenda of many organisational boards as well as a key performance indicator (KPI) for chief executives. These labour market trends have placed new importance on employment relationships and leadership, and have combined to profoundly affect career development for individuals and organisations.

It is broadly recognised today that leaders need to truly 'connect' with their employees in order to understand and support their professional and personal needs, recognising how these may change over time.

Effective leaders demonstrate authenticity in spades. They build trusted relationships by being open about their position while assisting others to be open about theirs. They appreciate and respect differing points of view and follow through on their commitments. Role modelling these behaviours is key to fostering connection and quality relationships. Employees should feel they can turn to you, as their leader, for objective career advice, and know it will always be in their best interests to do so.

Trust is the great enabler of learning. When trust is absent so too is learning, and both are critical to positive career development.

Moving from the old to the new career model

The traditional, paternalistic style of employment relationship, in which organisations were expected to manage their employees' careers, has long gone. In the contemporary career model, employees are considered free agents and loyalty is to the individual, not the organisation. Career development has evolved to become the responsibility of the individual.

Nowadays, progressive employers do not manage their employees' careers. They discuss career pathways and make available accessible career ladders and career development resources (such as coaching) to help employees achieve career clarity, identify career options and determine the best career direction for them.

The traditional career model of the last century was linear and one-dimensional. Young adults were encouraged to find a 'good job in a good company', nurture it and stick with it as long as possible, ideally until retirement. In his book *The Psychology of Careers* (1957), Donald Super discussed five life stages: *growth*, *exploration, establishment, maintenance* and *decline*. Super also talked about a *fantasy* sub-stage of *growth*, when stereotypically a boy dreamed of becoming a fireman, policeman or doctor while a girl imagined herself a ballerina or nurse (remember, this was a different era!). The *exploration* stage generally coincided with leaving school or, for some, taking up tertiary studies. Once employed and settled into a single organisation, usually for life, their career would pass through *establishment* (with *advancement* as a sub-stage) and *maintenance* stages, before winding down towards *decline* (*disengagement* and *retirement*). Figure 1.1 represents a greatly simplified version of a traditional linear model.

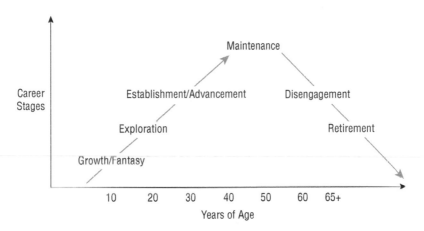

Figure 1.1: the traditional career model

Source: Adapted from D. E. Super (1957), *The Psychology of Careers*, Harper & Row, USA; and D. E. Super (1990), 'Life-span: Life-space approach to career development', in D. Brown, *Career Choice and Development* (2nd edn, Jossey-Bass, San Francisco, CA).

As an indication of the evolving nature of career development theory, Super much later referred to 'recycling' when discussing transitioning through his life/career stages.

Figure 1.2 represents a progressive, cyclical model that reflects a continuum of career exploration, engagement, growth, advancement, maintenance and disengagement over the course of a lifetime. Today's world of local and international career mobility has generated a career model in which many individuals can expect to 'recycle' and reinvent themselves through various career stages. Over their working life they can expect on average five careers and more than 15 jobs. Similarly, the traditional notion of retirement has given way to more flexible engagement options in the tertiary stages of career development.

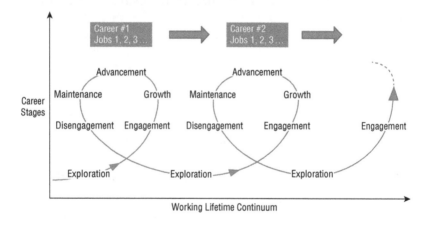

Figure 1.2: a contemporary 'recycling' careers model

Source: Adapted from D. E. Super (1957), *The Psychology of Careers*, Harper & Row, USA; and D. E. Super (1990), 'Life-span: Life-space approach to career development', in D. Brown, *Career Choice and Development* (2nd edn, Jossey-Bass, San Francisco, CA).

The traditional approach to career management assumed a paternalistic and 'transactional' style, rather than the more mature 'relational' employment relationship described by Denise Rousseau.

Transactional relationships were founded on limited emotional attachment. Organisations typically provided job security and material rewards in return for performance, conformity and loyalty. The employee's identity was linked directly to their skills and competencies.

Relational employment relationships are grounded in strong emotional attachment. They emphasise flexibility and personal accountability for performance in return for career rewards and development, with a long-term view in which the employee's identity is linked to the organisation. Both transactional and relational employment relationships relied on the acceptance of a basic social norm of reciprocal commitment or mutual obligation.

In the early to mid 1990s, the shift from *transactional* to *relational* work relationships had just begun, but was smashed apart when organisations embarked on widespread and large-scale downsizings. Many of the affected employees were well advanced in their careers, with tenures of 30 to 40 years or more. Back in the mid twentieth century, at 16 and looking for work, some had simply presented to the guardhouse of their nearest factory and asked for a job, any job! That was all that was required to get an immediate start for most factory work in those days. Many lacked formal qualifications and were ill equipped to transition to new careers after retrenchment. Subsequent research has shown that a third of these employees never worked again.

These events became a generational marker and changed the nature of employment relationships forever.

The children of the affected workers vowed not to let what had happened to their parents happen to them. The emerging generation of workers demanded a more adult form of relationship. The new relationship model included the imperatives of flexibility, a commitment to development and acceptance of them as free agents. This obliged organisations, and their leaders, to rethink their organisational frameworks and mindsets to accommodate a new, progressive form of employment relationship in order to attract and retain talent.

The new career reality

The new reality that has evolved today provides a plethora of exciting career opportunities. So what's the problem? It's simply this: many employees are unsure how to recognise or transition through the career stages of exploration, engagement, advancement, growth, maintenance and disengagement and on to a new career. Many just 'dust off' their résumé and start searching internet job boards when they feel a career move is needed. Just as problematic, many leaders don't know how to help them.

This is a challenge but also an exceptional opportunity for leaders, because it's never been more important than it is today to become skilled in helping employees enhance their career adaptability and agility.

Today's leaders are expected to actively demonstrate authenticity, transparency, agility and adaptability, and to be genuinely committed to their employees' career development. Leaders who only pay lip service to these traits and lack a focus on organisational career development are likely to be surrounded by subpar performers who are neither inspired nor motivated to improve themselves or their organisation. The red alert is that there's no faking it — employees can spot insincerity a mile off!

I have often heard leaders insist, 'We need to change the culture of this organisation.' It is also said that 'leaders get the culture they deserve', and in my experience this is spot on, because organisational culture mirrors leaders' behaviours. If leaders don't like what they see around them in their organisation, then they will need to take a long, hard and honest look at themselves before they can find the answers to what needs to change to produce the culture they're seeking. To attract and retain the best and brightest, leaders should look to their own values and behaviours first.

Employee experience — the new frontier of leadership

Employee experience has emerged as a key strategic focus for organisations seeking to fuel growth, as well as a source of sustainable competitive advantage. Some experts even believe employee experience is more important than customer experience — I now lean in this direction!

Like customer experience, employee experience is the sum of all interactions an employee has over their entire engagement with their employer. This includes everything from the pre-employment and induction stages through to departure. Bringing it off well requires all leadership sensory perceptions to be in high functioning order!

Employee experience is quite different from employee engagement, which has a narrower focus. Jacob Morgan, author of *The Employee Experience Advantage,* describes employee engagement as a 'short adrenalin shot' and employee experience as the 'long-term redesign of the organisation'. Morgan argues that employee experience should not replace employee engagement but coexist with it.

Ultimately, no matter how employee experience is defined, the evidence collected by researchers and other experts in this organisational field indicates that employee experience is fundamental to organisational prosperity in the short and long term.

Since employee experience owes a lot to effective conversations and career management throughout an employee's tenure, it figures that meaningful career conversations have a big role to play. In the chapters that follow I elaborate on how leaders can use and hone their sensory perceptions to enhance and drive career conversations.

Career coaching

Career coaching is a powerful tool that provides organisations with a practical approach to enriching engagement, retention, attraction and performance. It fosters positive and open employment relationships and enhances overall employee experience. Career discussions can also assist in improving role clarity, a lack of which can be a source of disharmony between colleagues that negatively affects their enjoyment of work. Moreover, many employees fear being held accountable for responsibilities they never knew they had!

Open, non-judgemental career discussions can help tease out potential role clarity issues, settling anxieties that may otherwise result in a decline in engagement and career satisfaction and subpar performance. This will become increasingly important as labour markets contort in order to sync with new work models.

A career development model

This model of career development, adapted from Judy Denham (2002), provides a useful context for understanding the key elements of career coaching (see figure 1.3). It highlights how each component interrelates with the others to provide a comprehensive and holistic framework for career development.

Figure 1.3: career development model

Source: Adapted from Judy Denham (2002), *Career Solutions* (www. careersolutions.com.au).

The right-hand side of this model deals mainly with career exploration, options analysis and goal setting, while the left-hand side focuses on action and implementation. Together, these elements make up an integrated approach to career coaching for today's leader.

Career satisfaction and competence

I have emphasised the importance of employee satisfaction in career development. Figure 1.4 (overleaf) illustrates the relationship between career satisfaction and competence, helping to identify what can, and can't, be traded off when considering career options and making career decisions.

Figure 1.4: elements of career satisfaction and competence

Career decisions fall into two main areas: *career satisfaction* elements (motivational, career, values and cultural beliefs fit) on the left side of the model and *competence* elements (skills, experience, behaviours, personality and cognitive attributes) on the right.

Some competence elements can be developed through skills training, formal education or behavioural training (technical skills and customer service, for example); other behavioural and attribute-based competencies, such as leadership resilience and emotional control, are better suited to development via coaching. Personality and cognitive attributes also indicate our behavioural preferences and can often be a valuable source of 'inferred' capability or potential in the absence of hands-on experience.

Career satisfaction elements, on the other hand, are largely rooted in our values and are therefore things that cannot be trained. We might also trade off *motivational fit* (what motivates you in the here and now) for longer-term *career fit*. For example, you may feel that although your job is not exactly what you want right now, the organisation is a good fit for the longer term and you can see a pathway to the right role.

Values and *culture fit* cannot be traded as easily, however, because these elements are the foundations of our belief system. If, after joining an organisation, an employee discovers it's a poor values or cultural fit for them, then usually the only remedy is to face up to it and move on. So to achieve career satisfaction employees' values and cultural belief systems must closely align with those of their employer.

Leaders will find that understanding the intrinsic differences between career satisfaction and competence elements will help untangle common confusions, such as the trainable and untrainable elements. It will also guide leaders in selecting the most suitable development interventions (procedural skill training, on-the-job training, behavioural coaching, career coaching and mentoring) for each employee. Understanding these elements and their differences will ensure career conversations begin and remain on a productive path.

Tips for leaders

Leaders have a unique opportunity to create an environment where career conversations, free of judgement and fear, are an intrinsic component of their relationship with their employees and protégés. However, as discussed, many leaders are not adequately prepared or skilled in this area of expertise.

This book introduces the essential skills and tools you will need to start and sustain an effective career conversation. If you follow this simple guide and commit to practising the techniques outlined here for the rest of your working life, you will be surprised by how easy it is to support your employees' careers and by the mutual benefits that follow. You will gain valuable insights not only into your employees but into yourself and your organisation.

Career leadership levers model

Finally, I developed this simple yet powerful model illustrating the essential career development levers that leaders can use to help their employees implement their career options and decisions (see figure 1.5).

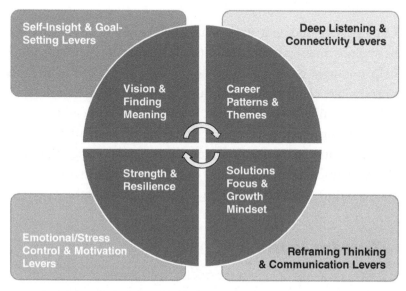

Figure 1.5: career development levers

Following is a brief description of these career development levers (their practical applications are discussed in further detail in later chapters).

SELF-INSIGHT AND GOAL SETTING

Developing self-insight is the key to finding personal meaning that's articulated by your vision of your career. This is then translated into corresponding goals that will drive your career towards your vision. Vision is the *why*: it encapsulates your core values, passions and dreams, and how you envision your future career and your life.

Goals translate your vision into specific actions. For example, your vision might be:

To make my career focus helping others achieve their potential and attain career satisfaction.

A corresponding specific goal to bring your vision to life could be:

Complete postgraduate studies part-time by setting aside 20 hours per week to master the theory and practice of leadership in career development and organisational development within two years.

Or,

Be appointed to a senior organisational development role in one of the top five logistics firms in the industrial sector within three years.

DEEP LISTENING AND CONNECTIVITY

Deep listening helps leaders to be acutely attuned to their employees and to correspondingly adjust their language to build trust, empathy and rapport to help identify career themes and patterns. This can help employees find what works for them and replicate this in their future career development.

EMOTIONAL/STRESS CONTROL AND MOTIVATION

Leaders can, and should, assist their employees to understand the importance of maintaining emotional and stress control as well as gaining insight into their intrinsic motivational drivers. This helps motivate employees to stay on track to achieve their goals and their career vision, particularly when facing challenges and obstacles.

REFRAMING THINKING AND COMMUNICATIONS

Reframing for a growth mindset and developing a solutions focus are great communication tools. They help leaders in challenging their employees to look at things differently in order to overcome obstacles and build confidence (even when they are not so sure!) and to find their way forward in their careers. This benefits employees (and leaders) in their professional and personal lives.

Summing up

The takeaway from this chapter is that leaders must be effective career coaches. This proficiency is an essential component of their overall leadership repertoire owing to a combination of three factors:

1. the changing model of careers and career development, and the role and attributes of contemporary career management in effective talent management

2. the high expectations of today's employees with regard to the quality and nature of their employer's leadership approach and capability

3. the necessity for organisations to provide enterprise-wide career development resources to assist employees to achieve career goals, work–life balance and satisfaction as a key component of their employee experience strategy.

Chapter 2
Reimagining careers

'Reality can be beaten with enough imagination.'
Mark Twain

Technology, artificial intelligence (AI) and automation are changing the nature of work so profoundly that the transformation could eclipse that brought on by the industrial revolution of the late eighteenth and early nineteenth centuries. We already see many signs of this. Robots are increasingly eliminating manufacturing jobs, and computer software is doing the job of thousands of office workers.

The introduction of automatic teller machines (ATMs) around the world wiped out countless banking jobs when they came into widespread use in the eighties. Today, some experts are forecasting that if your job *can* be automated, then it likely won't exist in five years' time. I think their five years might be optimistic and could reduce to three years or even less. What is certain is that there's a veritable, unstoppable tsunami of change coming at us!

The changing world of work

Developments in computer technology, big data, automation and AI suggest employers of the future may not need employees of the traditional kind but rather people with 'portfolio careers' who fulfil specific tasks or jobs as free agents. The online firm Airtasker is just one startup that is already servicing this need.

One might argue that given the rate of change that's expected to affect nearly every job, one way or another, talking about 'jobs' at all might be redundant, or of limited usefulness. We can catch glimpses of the technology horizon but we are yet to see the full horizon and all the opportunities it may bring to the world of work. Who knows what we will need employees to do and where we'll want them to do it in three, five or ten years' time? An often quoted claim has it that more than 65 per cent of future jobs have yet to be invented.

TRANSFORMING TECHNOLOGY

Technology is fuelling the growth of virtual companies. The proliferation of document-sharing and communication platforms and tools is enabling businesses to operate without the need for physical office space or a shared location.

CHANGING ATTITUDES AND NEEDS

Younger job applicants are looking for greater personal fulfilment and a better quality of life. Working remotely is fast becoming mainstream, and unsurprisingly it's not just younger workers who are expecting it. A 2017 study by Global Workplace Analytics and Flexjobs in the United States reported the average age of telecommuters (defined as those who work from home at least half of the time) as 46!

This was supported by Gallup's 2017 'State of the American Workplace' report, which identified the five criteria employees deem most important when they are considering a new job as:

1. the opportunity to do what they do best (60 per cent)

2. better work–life balance and personal wellbeing (53 per cent)

3. greater stability and job security (51 per cent)

4. a significant increase in income (41 per cent)

5. the opportunity to work for a company with a great brand or reputation (36 per cent).

JOBS AND THE GIG ECONOMY

The *gig economy* reflects the changing nature of employment, with the decline of full-time jobs and corresponding growth of part-time, temporary and short-term gigs. Career contractors and professionals pursuing portfolio careers have known of the opportunities and benefits of the gig economy for some time. This fundamental shift is predicted to filter through the entire labour market and become the norm rather than a labour market niche. Nobody really knows what proportion of the labour market the gig economy occupies today, largely because there is no consistent definition of a *gig* or reliable statistics to measure it, for that matter. However, some researchers believe today's gig economy to be around 10 per cent of the total employment market.

Implications for careers

The implications for careers are multifaceted and potentially dramatic. Office towers in our central business districts that currently house thousands of white-collar workers will likely be displaced by apartments in the next 10 to 15 years as these jobs yield to the growing wave of automation and AI.

According to a recent report from jobs website Adzuna Australia, a third of all jobs across Australia may be automated by the year 2030. While losses of old-world jobs are predicted to accelerate, new jobs are expected to emerge and soak up some of the discarded labour. Emerging job opportunities will benefit those with agile minds, skills and capability. Importantly, leaders can and should play a vital role in helping employees transition to the new jobs reality. One thing we can be certain of is that being flexible and adaptable will be a career imperative — indeed it already is!

It will necessitate a commitment to continuous learning and development. This, more than almost anything else, will equip employees to take advantage of emerging opportunities and to consider and make choices that may be beyond their current field of vision. Done well, it has the potential to build resilience and harmonise individual careers with employer needs. The die has been cast. The technological revolution will change the way in which humans add and create value. And leaders will be assessed on their ability to help their employees reach their individual and collective potential. This may be very different from how leaders look at building organisational capability today.

The art of reinvention

The rapidly changing world of work obliges employees to prioritise self-reflection as a career development imperative, not a 'nice to do'. This includes identifying transferable skills that are not discipline related, as well as isolating not only the skills they enjoy using, but those that align with current and future market needs. If this sounds simplistic or mere common sense, it's because it is. That said, you might be surprised by how many people are unaware of the benefits of these practices to successful career transition and development.

Leaders can help employees gain this insight and reap the career rewards that it yields. For some with extensive career experience, it may require that they *reinvent* themselves. For others who are just starting out on their career journey, it will mean matching career aspirations with the emerging employment trends. Both underline the need for doing your research. This may include pursuing qualitative and quantitative research in a way we've never had to do before.

Those with analytical minds may find research a natural and straightforward activity; others may find they have to really push themselves to do it in a focused and disciplined way. Here the imagination can play a critical role in stimulating progress. Einstein said, 'Imagination is more important than knowledge. For knowledge is limited, whereas imagination embraces the entire world, stimulating progress, giving birth to evolution.' Those who favour imagination over analysis can still achieve their career objectives, albeit by following a different path. A sure-fire winner for career success is a healthy combination of imagination and structured analysis. Whatever your preferred thinking style is, however, being thoughtful and purposeful in your approach to the market and your career is certainly a worthy goal.

Many labour market changes can be forecast with reasonable accuracy, so in most circumstances future events should not take us completely by surprise. It is possible to anticipate some changes that may affect your career by being alert, educating yourself, and researching history and trending issues. Such changes might include, for example, announced company restructuring, an economic shift, a change of government, and the growth or decline of industry sectors. Unfortunately, some prefer not to allow such precursors of career change to enter their thinking or field of vision. They understand the threat of these looming changes intellectually but opt to ignore them and react only when they happen.

MAKING CHOICES

We all make career choices, and how we action them will often determine our future. The key is to help employees avoid career paralysis and inertia out of anxiety driven by the fear of a lack of choices when confronted by unexpected or forced career change. I have found that carrying around a feeling of having limited choices can itself be debilitating and a career limiter.

This chapter emphasises the benefits of identifying and making choices based on the best information available while also using our imaginations. This means using our analytical and problem-solving skills to envisage opportunities in a world that will be quite different from the present one. It takes an open mind, a little research and courage to make that leap. Continuous learning (formal or informal) is a key enabler of career growth. One thing is certain: information is not in short supply today. It's never been easier to research just about anything, and better internet search engines and online research tools and resources continue to evolve.

Tips for leaders

Barack Obama, Bill Gates and Warren Buffett are just three examples of leaders who have embraced the idea of constant learning and reading. Leaders should encourage their employees to adopt the discipline of continuous learning as a fundamental foundation of their career development. Followers of the 'five-hour rule' (Gates and Buffett among them) commit to deliberate learning for at least five hours per week.

ROLE OF TRANSFERABLE SKILLS

Transferable skills enable active transitioning to new careers and roles. How exciting it is to imagine and ponder the unknown! Some skills, such as technically based ones, are specific to an industry or discipline. Many, however, can be adapted to new careers and are therefore regarded as 'transferable'. Examples of transferable skills include leadership, listening, numeracy, verbal, analytical, problem-solving, organisational and strategic planning. Transferable skills are a powerful advantage when adapting to emerging labour markets. Leaders need to be attuned to, and knowledgeable about, the potential of skills that can traverse many different occupations. Such adaptability is likely to grow in importance as technology drives the redundancy of existing jobs and their replacement with new roles, some of which, as discussed, are yet to be conceived.

Retraining and reimagining careers is, and will continue to be, a critical activity for leaders seeking to help their employees and protégés realign their careers to new realities.

No special magic is required to capture and leverage transferable skills. The first step is simply to be aware they exist; the second is to set about critically analysing which ones are relevant for the application. Next look at how they could fit and add value to different careers and industries. For example, leadership in its many forms is a highly adaptable transferable skill. It has been successfully applied across multiple platforms, no matter what the demands and changing needs of the market. As baby boomers exit the workforce and the growth of working-age populations in many Western countries slows to close to zero, leaders will face a renewed 'war for talent', a term first coined by McKinsey in the late nineties to describe organisational competition for talented employees. In this environment retraining will be essential.

In my experience, people who struggle to name their own transferable skills will display genuine excitement when you help them to identify a skill set they may have previously taken for granted. Since building capability is a key precursor to effective leadership, leveraging transferable skills is a critical part of the leader's toolkit not only now, but into the future.

Summing up

Reinventing yourself can be difficult and will draw heavily on creativity and resilience, particularly if labour market changes take you by surprise. Leaders have a big role to play in helping employees to work through anxieties fuelled by change.

I have learned that people do not fear change so much as *being changed*. Leaders can avoid losing valuable employees by helping them to imagine a different career within the organisation, by proactively supporting their career development and by empowering them to navigate new career pathways.

One longer-term retention strategy is to provide your talent with the freedom to leave and explore the wider world of work, with a formal undertaking to rehire them at a later date. Many leaders find this concept a little difficult to absorb. It does take courage and faith from both parties to make such a commitment, but, when executed well, it can be an extremely effective strategy as part of an organisation's overall workforce plan for building long-term capability.

Alan's career story

Alan had been a successful marketing executive for over 20 years and had worked for several multinationals in that time. Out of the blue, his current employer of 10 years took him completely by surprise by making his role redundant as part of a wider company restructure. Although Alan had known a restructure was imminent, he was shocked, as he had thought his role was safe. He just hadn't seen it coming.

Out of work, and with the phone unnervingly silent, over the following month or two Alan had time to gather his thoughts in the quiet of his study.

He had a long held interest in men's health and how to improve it. His previous roles had prevented him from pursuing this passion, but now he had time and energy to invest in research to determine whether he could transition this interest into a new career. With a generous severance package in the bank, he could comfortably survive financially without an income for 18 months.

Having practised marketing over many years, Alan had strong research capabilities, but he now needed to apply these skills in a different way. This time Alan's research was for himself and his career rather than for his employer. After intensive and multifaceted research over six months, he concluded that establishing a not-for-profit organisation would be the best way to promote men's health issues. He found a number of single-issue health initiatives but only a few organisations that promoted men's health overall, and these were not well known. Alan's marketing prowess now came to the fore. He could sense a compelling opportunity with a clear point of differentiation, and with this his business was born.

Alan began crafting a vision and strategy for his business. He knew how to do this very well from his discipline and corporate experience, but he still had much to learn about establishing a not-for-profit organisation. He further researched the not-for-profit sector to learn more about possible successes and failures and the reasons for each. To add to his knowledge bank he also enrolled in a short course that specialised in not-for-profit startups.

Eight months later Alan founded his company specialising in promoting men's health. He applied his leadership skills, strategic planning capability, business and commercial acumen, combined with his marketing expertise, research and newfound knowledge, to follow his passion. Alan's is a classic success story of transitioning to and navigating a new career. He used his innate creativity, applied his transferable skills to full advantage and undertook new training. With this thorough approach, supported by his innate energy and tenacity, he took a well-considered chance on a startup business that paid off in spades.

Key learnings

Alan's story is a classic case of building a new career from the ground up. Facing an uncertain future, he evaluated his options and created his vision and strategy. He applied his:

- » innate creativity skills
- » commercial and marketing skills
- » research skills
- » new training
- » transferable skills.

The story offers a master class on how to use a negative event (retrenchment) as a springboard to launch a totally new career while at the same time realising a long-held career dream.

Chapter 3
Fit your own mask first

'Be yourself; everyone else is already taken.'
Oscar Wilde

Airline passenger safety messages commonly instruct parents to fit their own oxygen mask before helping a child. It can feel counter-intuitive not to prioritise your children in an emergency, but you won't be able to help anyone else if you yourself are unconscious. In the same way, when helping others navigate their careers, the place to start is you!

Even if you are struggling with your own career goals, this does not preclude you from being effective in helping others with theirs. The most important thing is that you have the self-awareness to know where you are at. The better you know yourself and your own career drivers, the better equipped you will be to lead and help others with theirs.

A simple way to uncover your own career motivators is to review your career and identify your work-related values and career drivers. Chapter 4 includes exercises to help you in this (and to support your employees in doing the same). The aim is to identify connecting themes and patterns in your career journey to better understand how you make decisions and who or what might have influenced them. Discovering what drives your career progress will help you do the same for your employees. This is a vital first step. In documenting your career milestones, together with the outputs of these exercises, you may uncover an unexpected transition point.

Although there are many career assessment exercises available, I have found that using a narrative approach with employees is one of the most effective ways of helping them to recognise previous transition points, clarify their career direction and articulate clear career goals.

At first glance, retirement advice may seem an unlikely reference point for career development, but Kenneth Schultz, Megan Kaye and Mike Annesley's book *Retirement: The Psychology of Reinvention* has some illuminating messages for those in all stages of career development, from early to late career. Drawing on cognitive psychology, the authors explain how, consciously or unconsciously, we all follow a life script, using it to make sense of our experience. How we choose to interpret that script we have in our head is entirely up to us. 'Sometimes,' they suggest, 'we may generalise in a way that absolves us of blame for our own disappointments.'

Leaders should encourage their employees to tell their own story, to help them unpack and identify the key themes. They should not be reticent about challenging an employee's interpretation of the events that have led them to their current position. This is particularly important if the employee sees their experiences in a negative, unhelpful light or fails to identify critical aspects that have played a role in successes or failures in their career. In my experience, this is valuable not just for those in mid or late career with plenty of experience, but also for those in their early working life with limited career experience.

In sharing their story, guided by thought-provoking questions, employees will often experience a 'light bulb moment' when insight shines through the haze. In later chapters I will cover in more detail how to structure career conversations and goal setting. Despite my preference for taking a narrative approach to career conversations, I also include several assessment exercises in chapter 4. I have found these self-assessments among the most useful from the myriads available.

Where and how emotional intelligence fits

You will have heard plenty about emotional intelligence (EQ). For all that's been researched, written and discussed, I like to think of it simply in terms of *not letting your emotions stop you from achieving your goals*. That said, and as much as I like my simplistic definition, there is a good deal more to be gained from EQ, particularly from the standpoint of resonant leadership. Moreover, EQ capability and how to assess, develop and apply it have evolved significantly since its origins in the nineties.

According to psychologist and author Daniel Goleman, who popularised the EQ model in 1995, EQ is of much greater importance than IQ and technical skills for successful leadership.

In his book *The New Leaders,* Goleman argues that what he calls *primal leadership* is most effective when engaged in by emotionally intelligent leaders who by definition understand the power of creating resonance. Intellect alone is not enough. Intellect and emotions are controlled by different neural systems in the brain. The prefrontal-limbic circuitry controls our emotional intelligence competencies while the neocortex drives cognitive abilities such as technical skills.

Emotionally intelligent leaders also understand the negative impact that dissonance can have on teams and the organisation. I saw this powerfully demonstrated in one organisation I worked in where a poorly executed restructure took the organisation from solid resonance to unequivocal dissonance in a matter of weeks, with disastrous results. Resonance can be dismantled very quickly by errors of judgement or even a change of leadership. In this case, it took more than two years to re-establish trust and any form of organisational resonance. The senior leadership team responsible for the restructure were intellectually clever, but collectively lacked the EQ to 'read' the temperature and pulse of the organisation and therefore failed to adequately prepare it for the change process.

This example underscores how teams, as well as individuals, can benefit from becoming emotionally intelligent and why Goleman stresses the importance of developing empathy in order to develop resonance. Leaders must be self-aware and able to control their own emotions before they can deal with the emotions of others and truly 'connect'. Importantly, Goleman contends that EQ competencies can be learned. He identifies the four main EQ competence clusters as:

1. self-awareness
2. self-management
3. social awareness
4. relationship management.

Goleman also points to how humour, used wisely, can be an effective leadership tool and support the development of resonance. Laughter, he suggests, is a mostly spontaneous action. Its presence suggests, and reinforces, trust and openness.

Tips for leaders

Employing humour appropriately can be an effective communication tool for leaders. Throughout my leadership career I have found humour highly useful, particularly when defusing unproductive emotions arising from tense meetings. A word of caution, though: humour must be used thoughtfully and judiciously to avoid unintended consequences, such as perceptions that you are mocking or making fun of someone or trivialising their concerns. Alert, engaged, emotionally intelligent leaders know if, how and when it's appropriate to introduce humour into a discussion.

Intellectual, emotional and practical intelligence

I want to clarify the differences between intellectual, emotional and practical intelligence. Intellectual intelligence relates to our 'cognitive horsepower' and can be thought of as *academic intelligence*. Examples include analytical, creative and insightful thinking, all of which are skills required for effective leadership. Practical intelligence relies on tacit knowledge, which is knowledge that's learned through life experiences as opposed to in the classroom.

Emotional intelligence, on the other hand, is concerned with attributes that enable us to understand and manage our emotions to facilitate goal achievement. The research demonstrates overwhelmingly that EQ is a critical aspect of effective leadership.

In summary, emotionally intelligent leaders are self-aware and socially aware, and can control their emotions and manage relationships. It follows that your EQ capability will relate directly to your ability to hold effective career conversations.

Career coaching attributes, skills and knowledge

So what are the key attributes, skills and knowledge you need to master, as a leader, in order to guide and coach your employees in their careers? I have already touched on some of them, but here I'll offer a more comprehensive summary:

1. **self-awareness**—understanding self and having an interest in self-knowledge

2. **behavioural awareness**—showing insight into and understanding of others

3. **curiosity**—having innate interest in others and in supporting their development

4. **challenging skills**—inspiring personal change and transition

5. **agility**—being flexible and adaptable while keeping an open mind

6. **solution focused**—effective use of communication and listening skills

7. **EQ and relationship management**—building empathy and trust while managing appropriate personal boundaries

8. **maintaining perspective**—looking at the whole picture and keeping a realistic sense of proportion

9. **creativity and intellectual ability**—fostering diversity of thought, innovation and conceptualisation

10. **self-marketing**—being aware of the techniques (and risks) of personal branding and networking

11. **credibility**—displaying organisational and professional acumen, savvy and nous mediated by a healthy dose of humility!

12. **self-development**—role modelling a commitment to lifelong learning

13. **vision and goal setting**—demonstrated capacity to set goals and to stay focused and on track

14. **career management**—modelling an understanding of internal and external organisational career pathways and the broader world of work as well as familiarity with the use of basic career management tools

15. **ethics**—manifesting integrity and commitment to confidentiality.

Evaluation of coaching competencies

Take a moment to self-rate your career coaching skills and knowledge using table 3.1. In assessing your capability for each area, don't overthink each rating—just mark down the number that first comes to mind.

Table 3.1: assessing your career coaching skills

15 core career coaching skills rate yourself (1 = low, 5 = high)					
Self-awareness (understanding self)	1	2	3	4	5
Behavioural awareness (showing insight into others)	1	2	3	4	5
Curiosity (innate interest in others)	1	2	3	4	5

(continued)

Table 3.1: assessing your career coaching skills *(cont'd)*

15 core career coaching skills — rate yourself (1 = low, 5 = high)					
Challenging skills (inspiring personal change)	1	2	3	4	5
Agility (being flexible and adaptable)	1	2	3	4	5
Solution focused (communication and listening skills)	1	2	3	4	5
EQ and relationship management (building empathy and trust)	1	2	3	4	5
Maintaining perspective (looking at the whole picture)	1	2	3	4	5
Creative and intellectual ability (diversity and innovation)	1	2	3	4	5
Self-marketing (personal branding and networking)	1	2	3	4	5
Credibility (displaying professional acumen and savvy)	1	2	3	4	5
Self-development (commitment to lifelong learning)	1	2	3	4	5
Vision and goal setting (capacity to stay focused and on track)	1	2	3	4	5
Career management (career pathways and tools)	1	2	3	4	5
Ethics (integrity and commitment to confidentiality)	1	2	3	4	5

Don't worry if you find you have scored yourself poorly on some skills. If you're like most people it's likely you'll be tougher on yourself than others would be.

After completing this assessment, try asking yourself these questions and think about your answers:

» How would my peers and employees rate me?

» How might their assessments differ from mine?

The purpose of this assessment is to help you reflect on where you can improve your career coaching skills and knowledge. Incremental improvements, no matter how small, are beneficial; in a sense, the smaller the better, as they're the ones that are more likely to be achieved! For example, if you rate yourself a 1 on any scale, think of how you could move that up to a 2; if you rate yourself a 2, what might you do to move up to 3?

This simple self-evaluation is a great place for leaders to start building their capability to hold better career conversations with their employees. Chapter 4 outlines useful exercises to learn more about yourself as a leader in order to be better equipped to understand and help others find career clarity and direction.

Summing up

Emotionally intelligent leaders are self-aware and socially aware and are skilled at controlling their emotions and managing relationships. Your EQ capability will relate directly to your ability to hold effective career conversations.

As a leader you must understand the key attributes, skills and knowledge you need in order to guide and coach your employees in their careers. Such understanding provides a context for you to self-evaluate your career coaching skills, which is a great place to start for leaders wishing to build their leadership capabilities.

Marion's career story

Marion was the CFO of a large manufacturing firm. The company had recently restructured and changed its strategy and direction to counter increasing competition and market restructuring in their industry sector. This caused significant cash flow issues, which Marion and her team had been quietly managing.

Marion's direct report, Jack, was the senior management accountant. Jack, who has been with the firm for seven years, had recently begun voicing criticisms of the company. This fault-finding had unsettled other team members; even the newly appointed managing director had noticed Jack's critical demeanour.

Jack's behaviour caught Marion off guard. He had previously appeared to be settled in his career and was otherwise an exemplary employee, so she knew it was out of character. Her intuition told her that Jack's overt and at times over-the-top criticisms might signal a deeper issue.

Marion knew she had to talk to Jack to 'nip this issue in the bud', but she felt nervous about approaching him in his current state of mind. And she wasn't at all sure of how to bring his behaviour up with him in conversation, so for some time she procrastinated.

By way of background, around the time Jack's criticisms arose, Marion was adjusting to the leadership style of the newly appointed MD. This stressor, together with long working hours and the demands of her home life, undermined her enjoyment of work and led her to question her career direction.

As a senior manager, Marion understood the importance of maintaining emotional control and her executive disposition.

To help her navigate these challenges she decided she needed to consult an external mentor, a former CFO and now a skilled career coach. After a few sessions, Marion began to feel more settled and able to compartmentalise her own career concerns, and as a result she thought she was in a better position to help Jack.

Marion had previously enjoyed a good working relationship with Jack (or so she thought). Now she felt confident enough to approach him to ask what needed to be asked. She used simple questioning techniques designed to put Jack at ease, such as requesting his permission to ask about his concerns. To take the heat out of the moment and disarm Jack's natural oppositional reflex, she was empathetic, avoided judgement and acknowledged his emotions. Marion's conversation with Jack proved timely and her intuition correct, and Jack immediately warmed to his boss's approach. He soon opened up and shared that he was feeling unappreciated and taken for granted. Unable to see his next career step in the company, he had decided to resign.

Marion was shocked to hear that Jack felt this way, as she had thought she was providing ample recognition, feedback and leadership. Armed with this new insight, Marion was able to engage with Jack and, using behavioural examples, convince him that being antagonistic wasn't the best way to deal with his frustrations. So began a broad-ranging conversation around Jack's career achievements and drivers that was illuminating for them both.

Marion and Jack committed to establishing a written career development plan and to meeting each week to discuss his work and progress towards his career development goals.

Jack stayed with the company and reframed his criticisms into more helpful feedback offered in appropriate forums. Jack now has his career back on track and, importantly, feels his views are appreciated. What Jack didn't know was that the whole episode also helped Marion refocus on her own career satisfaction and development objectives.

Key learnings

Marion guided this positive outcome by:

- » trusting her intuition and engaging her innate EQ
- » being alert to other team members' reactions to Jack's behaviours
- » seeking the help of an external mentor to disentangle her own career concerns from those of others
- » asking open questions to help Jack open up about what was really troubling him
- » conducting a direct and deliberate career conversation with Jack using empathy and acknowledging his emotions, while being careful to avoid judgement (see also chapter 9).

Can you think of any additional leadership approaches Marion applied or initiatives she could have tried?

Chapter 4
Building career self-insight

'Yesterday I was clever, so I wanted to change the world.
Today I am wise, so I am changing myself.'
Rumi

We have discussed the value of self-awareness, including knowing what has shaped your career, values, and career drivers or motivators. Reviewing your own career will prove invaluable when helping others move towards their career goals.

This chapter provides some simple and quick techniques and exercises that will enable you to discover the key elements of your own career and provide a sound foundation for helping others do the same. There are a plethora of career assessment methods out there, but I have found the following techniques most valuable in assisting others to gain career clarity and focus.

A good place to start is to reflect on every career step you have made since leaving school and document each milestone on a timeline. As the saying goes, you can't navigate a ship by looking at its wake, but that said (and with apologies for the mixed metaphor!), checking the 'rear vision mirror' can help you visualise the future.

As you think back over your career, reflect on:

1. how you made each career move or transition

2. who influenced your decisions

3. when you were happiest in your career and what was going on for you at that time

4. whether your work-related values were satisfied in each role (the values exercise that follows will help you identify the most important ones)

5. the best and worst boss you ever had, and their attributes and leadership styles

6. how you like to be managed

7. who was the biggest influence in shaping your thinking and development, and what was their role and connection to you

8. your personal and professional networks, and how you used these network connections in your career development.

The next step is to look for emerging themes or patterns that have helped shape your career direction and decisions. Understanding what has worked for you in the past can provide valuable insights when planning future career moves and transitions.

The exercises in this chapter provide a 'metaphorical ruler' for evaluating opportunities or making career decisions by illuminating why some things simply don't feel right or why your 'gut feeling' conflicts with reality. We do this by clarifying your attributes, values, drivers and transferable skills.

Your attributes — your innate make-up

Your attributes are markers of your behavioural preferences—the ways you prefer to operate, especially when push comes to shove.

Review the list of attributes in figure 4.1 (overleaf) and circle all the ones you feel relate to you. Then select the six attributes you feel best describe your personality and behavioural preferences. For each of the six selected write a sentence or two in the table provided.

What we value really matters

Next, identify your key career values; remember, it's what *you* value and what you stand for. Values are what we stand for and also what we can't stand! For career satisfaction to be said to exist, at least your top four values are being satisfied, or have the potential to be satisfied, in your role and company. Below is a list of career values you may relate to. Are there others you can think of?

Circle all values listed in figure 4.2 (overleaf) that resonate with you, then select the eight that are most important to you and in the table rank those from one to eight (one being most important). Then write a sentence or two about what each of your top eight values means to you.

Achiever	Disciplined	Motivated	Self-controlled
Ambitious	Dynamic	Objective	Selfless
Aspiring	Energetic	Open-minded	Self-reliant
Assertive	Enterprising	Optimistic	Sense of humour
Calm	Enthusiastic	Organised	Sensitive
Candid	Entrepreneurial	Patient	Sincere
Caring	Flexible	Persistent	Sociable
Confident	Focused	Personable	Systematic
Constructive	Imaginative	Polite	Tenacious
Cooperative	Insightful	Practical	Thoughtful
Courageous	Intelligent	Realistic	Tolerant
Courteous	Kind	Reliable	Trusting
Creative	Leader	Resourceful	Trustworthy
Decisive	Loyal	Respectful	Wise
Determined	Mature	Responsible	
Diligent	Modest	Risk-taker	

Attribute	What this attribute means to me
1.	
2.	
3.	
4.	
5.	
6.	

Figure 4.1: career attributes

Accomplishment	Excitement	Problem solving
Adaptability	Expertise	Recognition
Advancement	Health and wellbeing	Respect
Aesthetics	Helping others / society	Risk-taking
Affiliation	Honesty	Routine
Authenticity	Humour	Search for meaning
Authority/power	Independence	Security
Autonomy	Influencing others	Self-determination
Belonging	Integrity	Self-fulfilment
Being different	Intellectual stimulation	Status
Change and variety	Interaction with public	Success
Collaboration	Job challenge	Supervision
Communication	Making decisions	Teamwork
Community	Material rewards	Tranquillity
Competitiveness	Morality	Work alone
Creativity	Participation	Work–life balance
Ethics	Physical demands	Zest

Career value	What this value means to me
1.	
2.	
3.	
4.	
5.	
6.	
7.	
8.	

Figure 4.2: career values

Career drivers survey

Career drivers are our key career motivators (and demotivators when not fulfilled). They point to sources of career satisfaction and dissatisfaction. They are *internal forces* that flow from our personality attributes, experience and values, and that can consciously or unconsciously help shape our career decisions.

This career drivers survey exercise is particularly valuable for employees who may be 'all at sea' with regard to their career direction and would benefit from a diagnostic tool to enhance awareness of their inner motivations. It can also help leaders and employees to identify career themes and patterns. This is useful when analysing and explaining how current and future satisfaction drivers can shape career decisions.

This exercise was adapted from a survey introduced in Dave Francis's book *Managing Your Own Career*. In my experience, we need at least our top three or four career drivers to be present to feel a sense of satisfaction in our working life. Without these career drivers, you may feel something is missing in your career yet not be able to put your finger on what it is.

SURVEY COMPLETION INSTRUCTIONS

Table 4.1 lists 36 pairs of statements about what you might want from your career. Assess each pair of statements, allocating a total of three points between them according to their relative importance to you. You might, for example, give one statement two points and the other one point, or you might give one statement three points and the other zero.

Tip for leaders

Don't overthink your score weighting—just pick what seems right to you. Sometimes you may find yourself struggling to preference one statement over another, but this is all part of the exercise, which is designed to compel you to choose one statement and not sit on the fence! There are no right or wrong selections, just what feels right for you given your preferences.

Table 4.1: career drivers survey

No.	Statement	Letter	Score
1	I will need an uncommonly high standard of living to feel fulfilled.	A	
	I want to have a significant influence over others.	B	
2	I only feel content if the work I do has value.	C	
	I want to be an expert in everything I do.	D	
3	I want to be creative at work.	E	
	It is important to me to work with people I like.	F	
4	I want to be free to choose what I do.	G	
	I want to ensure my financial security.	H	
5	I like the feeling that people look up to me.	I	
	Ultimately I want to be wealthy.	Λ	

(continued)

Table 4.1: career drivers survey *(cont'd)*

No.	Statement	Letter	Score
6	I want a significant leadership role.	B	
	I focus on what is meaningful to me, rather than what pays well.	C	
7	I want to feel like my expertise was hard-won.	D	
	I want to create things that people will associate solely with me.	E	
8	I want good social relationships with my colleagues.	F	
	I want to decide how I spend my time.	G	
9	I will not be satisfied without lots of material possessions.	A	
	I need to satisfy myself that I know my job well.	D	
10	My search for meaning in life is bound up in my work.	C	
	I want the things I make to carry my name.	E	
11	I want to earn enough to buy anything I want.	A	
	I want a job that offers long-term security.	H	
12	I want a role that allows me to influence others.	B	
	My goal is to be a specialist in my field.	D	

No.	Statement	Letter	Score
13	I want to make a positive contribution to the wider community.	C	
	I value close relationships with other people at work.	F	
14	I want a role in which I can be creative.	E	
	I want to be my own master.	G	
15	I like working closely with others.	F	
	I want to be confident that my position will remain secure in the future.	H	
16	I want to be able to spend money freely.	A	
	I want to be innovative in my work.	E	
17	I enjoy telling others what to do.	D	
	I enjoy being close to others.	F	
18	My career is bound up in my search for greater meaning in life.	C	
	I want to be responsible for making my own decisions.	G	
19	I want to be known as a specialist.	D	
	I need a secure career path to feel relaxed.	H	
20	I want to enjoy the symbols of wealth.	A	
	I enjoy meeting new people through work.	F	

(continued)

Table 4.1: career drivers survey *(cont'd)*

No.	Statement	Letter	Score
21	I like having oversight over how others perform.	B	
	I like to choose for myself the tasks I undertake.	G	
22	To fully commit myself to a role, I need to feel the results are worthwhile.	C	
	I would like very much to know where I will stand on retirement.	H	
23	Close work relationships make it hard for me to make a career change.	F	
	It's important to me to be accepted as part of the 'Establishment'.	I	
24	I would like to be in charge of people and resources.	B	
	I want to make things no-one else has made.	E	
25	I do what I think is important, not what aids my career.	C	
	I want to be publicly recognised.	I	
26	I want to do something quite different from what others do.	E	
	I usually opt for the safest course of action.	H	
27	I like others to look to me for leadership.	B	
	Social status often influences my judgement.	I	

No.	Statement	Letter	Score
28	A high standard of living appeals to me.	A	
	I dislike being tightly controlled by a manager.	G	
29	I want what I produce to bear my name.	E	
	I want my achievements to be formally recognised by others.	I	
30	I like to be in charge.	B	
	I am uncomfortable when I cannot see very far ahead at work.	H	
31	I want to have specialist knowledge that is valued.	D	
	I prefer not to be answerable to other people.	G	
32	I dislike being a small cog in a large wheel.	G	
	I would like a high-status job.	I	
33	I am prepared to work more for material reward.	A	
	I see work as a pathway to personal development.	C	
34	I want my role to carry prestige.	I	
	I'm most attracted by a secure future.	H	
35	So long as my co-workers are also my friends, nothing else matters.	F	
	I like being able to make expert contributions.	D	

(continued)

Table 4.1: career drivers survey *(cont'd)*

No.	Statement	Letter	Score
36	I would enjoy the status of a senior position.	I	
	I want to use my specialist knowledge in a highly competent way.	D	

Source: Based on a survey from *Managing Your Own Career* by Dave Francis (1985).

SELF-SCORING YOUR CAREER DRIVERS SURVEY RESULTS

Now transfer the points you have given to each letter item in the designated box in table 4.2. The total should be 108; if not, check your arithmetic!

Table 4.2: career drivers results

Letter item	Points allocated to each letter item								Total for letter item
A									
B									
C									
D									
E									
F									
G									
H									
I									
Grand total									108

YOUR CAREER DRIVERS PROFILE

Now this is the exciting part! It's time to view your results by plotting your career driver scores for each letter on the chart in figure 4.3. Circle the numbers you scored for each letter, then join them up to create a graphic profile of your personal career drivers.

24	24	24	24	24	24	24	24	24
23	23	23	23	23	23	23	23	23
22	22	22	22	22	22	22	22	22
21	21	21	21	21	21	21	21	21
20	20	20	20	20	20	20	20	20
19	19	19	19	19	19	19	19	19
18	18	18	18	18	18	18	18	18
17	17	17	17	17	17	17	17	17
16	16	16	16	16	16	16	16	16
15	15	15	15	15	15	15	15	15
14	14	14	14	14	14	14	14	14
13	13	13	13	13	13	13	13	13
12	12	12	12	12	12	12	12	12
11	11	11	11	11	11	11	11	11
10	10	10	10	10	10	10	10	10
9	9	9	9	9	9	9	9	9
8	8	8	8	8	8	8	8	8
7	7	7	7	7	7	7	7	7
6	6	6	6	6	6	6	6	6
5	5	5	5	5	5	5	5	5
4	4	4	4	4	4	4	4	4
3	3	3	3	3	3	3	3	3
2	2	2	2	2	2	2	2	2
1	1	1	1	1	1	1	1	1
0	0	0	0	0	0	0	0	0
A	B	C	D	E	F	G	H	I
Material rewards	Power and influence	Search for meaning	Expertise	Creativity	Affiliation	Autonomy	Security	Status

Figure 4.3: personal career drivers profile

You will notice that each letter now has a label (*Material rewards, Power and influence,* etc.). Now join the dots of each score. You will most likely have a squiggly line with peaks and troughs. Your chart may show wide score variations between drivers or only small ones. Either way is fine; remember, there are no right or wrong results, only what feels right for you.

Select your top four career drivers (the drivers with the highest numerical scores) and enter them into table 4.3. Then write a sentence or two about what each one means to you.

Tip for leaders

If you have identical scores for more than one driver, then select which you feel is most important to you or increase your top drivers to five or six.

Table 4.3: top four career drivers

Top four career drivers	What this driver means to me
1.	
2.	
3.	
4.	

Take a look at the following descriptors for each career driver. Did your survey results resonate with your self-perceptions before doing this exercise? Did they hold any surprises?

CAREER DRIVER DESCRIPTORS

Dave Francis summarised descriptors for each of the nine career drivers he identified for this survey as shown in table 4.4.

Table 4.4: the nine career drivers

Driver	What you are seeking
Material rewards	Wealth and possessions
Power/influence	Control over people and resources
Search for meaning	Opportunity to do things of value for their own sake
Expertise	High accomplishment in a specialised field
Creativity	Recognition for original, innovative work
Affiliation	Enriching relationships with others at work
Autonomy	Independence in key decision making
Security	A stable, dependable future
Status	Recognition, respect and admiration from others

IDENTIFYING YOUR SKILLS

This exercise will help you to identify skills, importantly the skills you most like using. For example, I am really good at numerical analysis. When others know that, they try to get me doing it, but I don't like using that skill so I keep it a secret! Figure 4.4 (overleaf) lists skills related to capabilities that are regarded as transferable to new work environments. Tick each skill in which you would rate yourself as proficient.

Manual/technical skills

☐ Assemble/install

☐ Construct/build

☐ Fix/repair

☐ Reason mechanically

☐ Work with animals

☐ Use hand tools

☐ Operate machinery and equipment

☐ Landscape/garden

☐ Manual dexterity

Analytical/problem-solving skills

☐ Analyse/diagnose

☐ Research/investigate

☐ Analyse data/finances

☐ Classify/organise

☐ Evaluate/assess

☐ Communicate scientifically/technically

☐ Reason logically

☐ Reason mathematically

☐ Use facts

☐ Prioritise

Figure 4.4: transferable skills

Innovative skills

- ☐ Innovate/invent something new
- ☐ Design graphically
- ☐ Use intuition
- ☐ Design programs, events
- ☐ Develop ideas
- ☐ Act/perform
- ☐ Write creatively
- ☐ Brainstorm
- ☐ Have artistic sense
- ☐ Draw/design artistically
- ☐ Synthesise facts creatively
- ☐ Compose music

Social/interpersonal skills

- ☐ Listen skilfully
- ☐ Develop rapport/understanding
- ☐ Coach/guide/advise/mentor
- ☐ Empathise/interview
- ☐ Instruct/train/educate
- ☐ Put others at ease
- ☐ Facilitate groups
- ☐ Cooperate/collaborate with others
- ☐ Heal/nurse/nurture

(continued)

Leading/managing/influencing skills

- ☐ Administer programs/resources
- ☐ Lead/coach
- ☐ Direct/supervise
- ☐ Make decisions
- ☐ Negotiate
- ☐ Sell/persuade
- ☐ Supervise/lead programs, projects, activities
- ☐ Set goals
- ☐ Organise and manage activities

Detail/data skills

- ☐ Work with numerical data
- ☐ Proofread/edit
- ☐ Inspect/examine
- ☐ Data entry
- ☐ Follow direction accurately
- ☐ Complete details on schedule
- ☐ Keep track of data/numbers
- ☐ Categorise/sort
- ☐ Remember numbers/specific facts
- ☐ Attention to detail
- ☐ File/classify/record/retrieve

Figure 4.4: transferable skills (*cont'd*)

For the skills in which you are proficient, use table 4.5 to identify those you most enjoy using and those you would prefer not to use.

Table 4.5: your most and least preferred skills

Most enjoy using	Prefer not to use

Now you have determined your attributes, career values, career drivers, transferable skills, key milestones and influences over your career span, summarise these in table 4.6 (overleaf).

Table 4.6: your top attributes, values, drivers and skills

Top 6 attributes selected	1
	2
	3
	4
	5
	6
Top 8 career values	1
	2
	3
	4
	5
	6
	7
	8
Top 4 career drivers	1
	2
	3
	4
Skills/ proficiencies most enjoyed	
Key career milestones	
Career highlights	
Key career influences	
Career themes identified	

Tip for leaders

To assist in synthesising this information, answer these questions:

1. What have you learned?

2. Did anything surprise you?

3. Are at least your top four or five career values being satisfied or potentially satisfied in your current role or company?

4. How could this help others?

5. Are you more in control of your career than you thought, even though you have tended simply to take up opportunities as they arise?

6. Even though it might have looked like chance, could you have really been working to a plan without realising it?

7. If you had reflected on your career sooner, would it have changed any decisions you have made so far?

Personal SWOT analysis

You may also find it useful to complete a personal Strengths, Weaknesses, Opportunities and Threats (SWOT) analysis. A SWOT analysis is most commonly used by organisations during their strategic planning, but it's just as useful for individuals when career planning.

Complete table 4.7 (overleaf). Begin by brainstorming everything that comes to mind under each category and refine your SWOT from there. Don't overthink your inputs, and don't forget to review the outputs of the other exercises in this chapter for inspiration!

Table 4.7: your personal SWOT analysis

Your personal strengths *For example, leadership capability.*	**Your personal weaknesses** *For example, a lack of formal qualifications in the field.*
Career opportunities *For example, the growth of the healthcare sector.*	**Threats to your career** *For example, age discrimination.*

Consider ways you might neutralise or mitigate the threats you have identified.

Letter from the future

If an employee is finding it difficult to articulate what they want and continues to feel 'stuck' no matter what approach you use, then ask them to write a 'letter from the future'. Anthony Grant first introduced me to this exercise early in my coaching practice, and I have had considerable success with it. I present the gist of it here, but if you want to read more about it, I recommend his book *Coach Yourself: Make Real Changes in Your Life*.

This is how it works.

Ask your employee to list half a dozen negative aspects of their career that they are merely 'tolerating' right now. Then ask them to imagine or visualise a time in the future (nine or twelve months is often a useful time frame) when they are no longer experiencing these problems and are enjoying career clarity, enjoyment and satisfaction.

Ask them to write a letter to you describing what things are like for them at this point in the future. What does their new reality look like and how do they feel? Have them use as much colour and detail as possible to bring this future to life.

As a thought starter to guide them, suggest they shape their story around how they arrived at their new positive reality. They should include their triumphs and achievements, as well as any obstacles or challenges they encountered along the way, and how they got over them to arrive at this 'better' career place.

It's not important how long the letter is — it could be one page or 20 pages. Your purpose is to help 'stuck' employees get unstuck and move forward. It is one more way to assist in overcoming procrastination, finding career direction, building motivation and effectively beginning to articulate goals, which you can help them to refine into SMART goals, as discussed in chapter 6.

Summing up

Understanding what has helped shape your own career gives you a greater appreciation of how to help your employees. You may find that some or all of the exercises described in this chapter will enrich your career conversations with employees.

The exercises will be particularly valuable for employees who are 'all at sea' with their career or simply seeking confirmation about their current direction. They provide the foundations for helping employees craft their vision for their career, set goals and move towards their career aspirations.

Daniel's career story

Daniel came to me seeking career coaching. Though he was performing well as a financial analyst, he was miserable and felt he badly needed a change of career. The problem was he didn't know to what!

Daniel had been in his current role for eight years. He liked his employer, but his boss lacked the interpersonal and leadership skills needed to engage Daniel in a career discussion. He had always received excellent performance reviews, but his career and development needs were never addressed.

Daniel didn't feel comfortable discussing his unhappiness in the job with his manager, so he sought my help, having been referred to me by a mutual associate who knew of my work in the executive and career coaching field.

Daniel was highly motivated to find career satisfaction so was keen to get working with me straight away. I began by helping him review his career using a narrative approach. This proved valuable in highlighting the themes and key influencers in Daniel's career journey all the way from when he left school through to the present day.

It turned out that Daniel had historically allowed others to direct his career, opting for a passive approach, taking up opportunities only as they presented. While relating his career story Daniel had a 'light bulb moment', realising he had been willing to leave his career decisions to others despite nagging feelings of doubt and unhappiness with his overall career direction. Daniel decided things needed to change. From now on, he vowed, *he* would decide what was best for his career and not leave it to others. Having had this epiphany, Daniel needed to know what career satisfaction would look like and how to achieve it, and he was more motivated than ever to work this out.

I had Daniel complete the attributes, career values, career drivers and transferable skills exercises. Not surprisingly, his results showed that although his values closely matched those of his company, his career fit was left wanting. His career drivers emphasised his motivation was geared towards creativity, search for meaning and affiliation, rather than the expertise and autonomy needed in his current and previous analytical-oriented roles. To his surprise, Daniel also found he had a number of transferable skills he really enjoyed using, such as innovating, designing, training and coaching.

These insights provided a valuable base to brainstorm possible career options both within and outside his current organisation. With this information in hand Daniel then researched each option and, with my help, evaluated each one against his key satisfaction criteria and 'metaphorical ruler'. He then set several corresponding SMART career goals (discussed further in chapter 6).

Daniel was excited to learn through his research about his employer's creative and design department. What's more, he discovered that this department was planning to recruit for a newly created role suited to someone with a technical background whom they could train in creative design. Bingo! The next step was for Daniel to approach his manager and open up about his career aspirations and desire to investigate this new internal opportunity with the department head.

Daniel's newfound self-insight gave him the confidence to speak to his boss forthrightly, from an informed position, about why he was seeking a career transition. Although at first Daniel had been apprehensive about approaching his manager he found that when he did so he was very supportive. His manager explained that he had been aware for some time of Daniel's dissatisfaction in his role but was unsure about how to discuss it with him.

Daniel applied for the role and was successful. He found a strong career fit with his current employer, while the company retained a highly valuable and talented employee. A win–win outcome! Daniel was delighted. He is confident his career is now on the right track and moving towards his career goals and satisfaction.

Key learnings

An employee who is dissatisfied in their role and looking for another challenge may find that the answer is right under their nose, in a different role in their existing organisation. This option offers a win–win for the employee and the organisation. It also highlights:

» the value of basic career analysis, research and options evaluation
» how education and training can build on transferable skills to support a positive internal career change.

Chapter 5
What's your personal brand?

'At the centre of your being you have the answer: you know who you are and you know what you want.'
Lao Tzu

Whether we like it or not we all have a brand. Our brand differentiates us from all others. Fortunes are often shaped by perceptions of our brand, whether those perceptions are accurate or inaccurate.

Social media can play a big role in creating perceptions of our personal and professional lives, and in painting a true or misleading picture of who we are. Our many and varied personal interactions also create impressions of our persona.

Useful questions to consider are:

- » Who are you?

- » What do others think of you, and are they right?

- » How would you describe yourself and how would others describe you?

» If your brand could talk, what would it say?

» How do you connect with people's emotions, hopes and dreams?

Your personal brand is powerful and can play an important role in your career opportunities and pathways. What may seem like *happenstance* (discussed in chapter 10) could be your personal brand at work. And your brand often precedes you. Most people will only ever experience a perception of you through your brand, rather than experiencing you personally. Similarly, communities, such as your workplace or industry, will form a collective (and often lasting) view of your brand that can influence people's perception of you. This may impact what career opportunities are available to you.

Building and nurturing our personal brand is essential for career development. Leaders, as well as mentors and trusted advisers, can play a key role in helping their employees establish, protect and promote their personal brand, and moving them towards their career objectives.

Networking — a powerful tool

Networking is a powerful tool when establishing, protecting and promoting your personal brand. Connecting with your network may be by phone, email, social media or face to face, or most likely a combination of all of these. The *tipping point*, an idea popularised by Malcolm Gladwell in his book of the same name, refers to the point at which a series of incremental changes reaches critical mass so that an idea, trend or social behaviour really takes off. We see this phenomenon at work in networking: you can work your network relentlessly for no apparent gain until suddenly, as if by magic, your efforts hit a tipping point and opportunities abound. Networks need to be constantly fed and nourished, though. This means proactively, regularly and persistently reaching out in a way that adds value for both you and your contacts.

First, however, you need to establish who is in your network. Writing a list of all your professional and personal network connections is a good place to start. You may be surprised by how extensive your network is already! Arguably, face-to-face meetings are the most powerful way of building your brand, though social media tools such as LinkedIn are extremely valuable too. Social media is like a 'silent army' working on your behalf, 24/7.

A global survey conducted by LinkedIn in 2017 found that almost 80 per cent of professionals believe networking to be important to career success. As with any networking activity, your social media profile and brand need constant nourishment. Start with a solid LinkedIn profile and headline. A quick web search will reveal a number of excellent sites showcasing the key ingredients of a good LinkedIn profile and headline with plenty of examples.

LinkedIn also provides real-time online feedback on the strength of your profile. A strong profile and a carefully targeted headline will not only support your brand but determine how you will be discovered via online searches. Don't fall into the trap of recycling your résumé in your LinkedIn profile. Your résumé outlines your career history, education and achievements; your LinkedIn profile is an opportunity to give readers a sense of *you*—what drives you, your passions and how these link to your vocation, past, present and future. It's an opportunity to open a window on your professional soul and establish a 'connection' with the reader. Never write your LinkedIn profile in the third person!

With a personal, carefully crafted profile and headline, you might be surprised who reaches out to you, whether an old, lapsed connection or a new contact who might be helpful to your career. A word of warning, though. While social media can be your best friend, it can also be your worst enemy if you don't manage what you post carefully. Rightly or wrongly, others will form views of you based on what you post on social media. Think, before you hit the 'post' button, will this support or hinder my brand? An unwise one-off post may come back to haunt you when you least expect (or afford) it, perhaps years later. A personal, seemingly harmless post may be dredged up long afterwards to sabotage, for example, an aspiring political career. Remember, post anything anywhere online and it remains in cyberspace forever!

The very subject of networking can cause anxiety when raised in a career discussion, yet it is fundamental to self-promotion and -development. Those wishing to promote their career through networking sometimes worry about imposing on those they approach, whether work associates or family and friends. In most cases, though, your connections will be pleased to hear from you and happy to help you if they can. It will work to your advantage and help nurture your network contacts if you stay in touch with them when you *don't* want or need anything.

Look for opportunities to share with your network information that may be of mutual interest—an article, blog post or book title, for example. Setting up a regular time in your diary each week or month for networking is a rewarding discipline.

Many people I have coached who were apprehensive about networking at first later shared how easy and enjoyable they found this activity once they took the plunge. Leaders can play a critical role in helping employees overcome their fear of networking by encouraging them to include it in their regular routine as part of their ongoing career development. We can do this by role modelling and sharing case studies of how others have used networking to advance their careers.

Tips for leaders

When talking to leaders about corporate culture, I often share the saying, 'You get the culture you deserve'. As a leader, if you don't like the culture you see, then take a good look at yourself because it almost certainly mirrors your own behaviours and values. Whether or not they know it or like it, leaders set the tone in the company.

In the same way, it is up to you as an individual to cultivate and drive your brand. No-one wakes up with the thought, 'What can I do for someone else's brand today?' The bottom line is, if you don't like what you or others see, then do something about changing it! You can be sure that if you don't, others won't either. It's up to you and only you. The key message for leaders is to take responsibility for the culture they create and help their employees to find and develop their professional identity and brand.

Mentors can help

Mentors can also help expand networks by introducing mentees to their networks and demonstrating, in practical terms, how they have used networking to promote and develop their own careers.

I am often asked, 'Is there a difference between coaching and mentoring?' The answer is a resounding yes! A *mentor* may conjure up a mental image of an old man with a white beard in flowing robes, whereas a *coach* can evoke an image of someone in a tracksuit with a stopwatch in their hand observing a top athlete. In an organisational context, mentors focus on sharing their greater experience and depth of knowledge of the mentee's industry or employer. Coaching is a facilitative and collaborative process. The coach uses an 'ask, not tell' approach to help the coachee identify and achieve their goals. Knowledge of the coachee's industry or organisation is not required, as the coach's skills lie in their ability to facilitate movement towards personal and professional development and goal attainment.

In my experience, the best mentors are also skilled coaches, though such individuals are hard to find! Usually, however, there is no shortage of executives who are only too happy to share their wisdom and experience with younger aspirants.

Mentors can be found internally, within the organisation, or externally. There are advantages and disadvantages in each case. Either way, confidentiality is paramount. Internal mentors may have a stronger understanding of the organisation. However, some find it more comfortable opening up to an external mentor who sits outside the politics of their organisation. In either scenario, since the mentor's only role is to help and support their mentee's success, few fail to benefit from the exchange! A number of organisations now offer formal mentoring programs. This is a great opportunity for leaders to play a supportive role in their employees' professional development. Alternatively, employees can source their own mentor independently.

While mentoring has been discussed here in the context of networking, it has the potential to propel an employee's overall career and should be prioritised in the suite of career development activities.

Summing up

When it comes to personal branding, perceptions are everything. We cannot control everything that is thought, said and written about us, but we are responsible for constructing our brand and deciding how to communicate it. If we leave it to others to define our brand image, then we effectively abdicate this responsibility and may end up being perceived quite differently from how we would wish.

The key message for leaders is to take responsibility for the culture they create and to help their employees to find, develop, own and protect their professional identity and brand.

George's career story

George had been in the glass production industry for more than 20 years. Over that time he climbed from sales administrator to the most senior sales management position in his company and industry. He excelled in every role he had and took advantage of every opportunity that presented. George had only one interview in his 20-year tenure and that was for his first role. He now led the entire sales division.

George was a university dropout who, as he puts it, 'fell into' his career. He had no time for studies as his career trajectory was steep and involved a constant whirlwind of activity and responsibilities. When he was 49 years old a new CEO arrived with different ideas from his predecessor about how to fix the company's flagging fortunes. The new man immediately sidelined George, along with a number of other long-serving executives who had built the company to where it was today. He believed a new executive team was needed, and George was fired soon after.

George's ego and self-esteem were hit hard. For the first time in his working life he found himself unemployed, and he was overcome by a sense of helplessness and inadequacy. The gravity of unemployment weighed on him like a tonne of bricks. On top of this, he had to contend with an employment market that was going through a tough patch and where age discrimination was rife. Old friends were silent, as was his phone. George was embarrassed by what had happened. He also felt isolated, abandoned and alone. Although historically the company's perception of him had been positive, the new CEO saw him as one of the 'old guard', incapable of leading the sales team in a new direction.

Reaching out to his old contacts, George learned that the new CEO's perception of him had spread through the broader glass industry. As a result, the unsolicited offers of employment that he had been accustomed to receiving completely dried up. He applied for literally hundreds of jobs only to be met with rejection letters and indifference. He was 'screened out' of contention, in many instances without so much as an interview, sometimes as a result of his lack of academic qualifications.

George became more and more despondent. His network, some of whom were fearful for their own positions, reaffirmed how tough things were for people at his age with experience but no formal qualifications. Finally, George came to recognise that he had to reinvent and rebrand himself. This was a pivotal moment in his career. With the local glass manufacturing industry in decline, it became increasingly clear that he would have to chart a different course and target a different industry sector. To do this, he concluded he needed to leverage and market his transferable skills to another industry, but first he had to figure out what his transferable skills were!

George asked a previous colleague with career management skills to help him identify and prioritise his transferable skills. He then set about approaching his network to glean information on growth industry sectors that were in need of his skills and that were consistent with his experience, capability and career objectives. When he actively put himself in the market, much to his surprise he found his contacts were happy to help him. They were genuinely interested in what he was doing.

The more George networked, the more he came to appreciate that his network connections, some of whom were concerned about their own career instability, were also interested in what they could learn about the market from his networking activity. He found the benefits of network meetings were mutual—a win–win situation!

George discovered that some connections were simply curious, even plain nosy, about his version of the events leading to his termination. He was smart enough to know the potential brand damage that could be caused by being drawn into a 'company bagging session' so he deflected such questions by shifting the conversation to his forward career goals. If this line of questioning persisted, he made sure he didn't say anything that could be perceived as critical of his previous employer. He would say, for example, 'The new CEO has a perfect right to pick his own executive team, and unfortunately that didn't include me.'

One of George's responses was, 'I really enjoyed my 20 years with the firm and although I'm sorry to leave, I have made many friends. I was afforded excellent professional development along with a number of fabulous career opportunities in my time there. The company also looked after me with a generous termination package.' In all instances, he ensured that he spoke only positively about his time with the company, including around his departure.

George got a real confidence boost when his networking activity started paying dividends. This gave him the energy, especially on the tough days, to keep going. A major milestone was passed when he realised that the loss of his job was the catalyst to reinvent and rebrand himself. His new posture to the market projected a positive, progressive, relevant and talented executive with highly transferable skills such as leadership, strategic planning and building organisation capability.

Determined not to let his lack of formal qualifications be a limiting factor again, he enrolled in Master of Business Administration. George's revised personal brand and approach to the market made a powerful value proposition for organisations facing change. With this renewed vigour and vision, George found it easy to present to others with a positive outlook rather than allowing the negative aspects of his departure to define him. He took charge of defining how he wanted himself and his career achievements to be perceived.

Through persistence and application, George found his new career move eight months later. His network advocated for his repositioned brand proposition and redefined career goals, and helped him to find a senior leadership opportunity in the logistics industry. Armed with a positive career focus and a clear value proposition, George secured the role over a number of rivals with direct industry experience. The hiring company were quick to see how George's transferable skills, experience and capability could be adapted to help transform their troubled courier business.

George has never looked back. Five years on he continues to enjoy career success and satisfaction in his new company. However, he hasn't forgotten the lessons learned from taking direct control of his own career and the importance of continuing to actively and systematically nurture and manage his brand and network. George is now using the insights gained, particularly during this career transition, to mentor others—and he's enjoying every minute of it!

Key learnings

George's career story points to the importance of:

» taking direct control of your own career
» continuing to actively and systematically nurture and manage your personal brand and network
» recognising the value the insights a mentor with previous experience of career transitions can offer.

Chapter 6
The goal of goal setting

'Know what you want to do, hold the thought firmly, and do every day what should be done, and every sunset will see you that much nearer the goal.'
Elbert Hubbard

Vision, articulated through goals and objectives, is the embodiment of values, purpose and meaning. It says you are what and where you want to be. While some start this process at a young age, most will not be able to develop a clear view of their career until adulthood. This chapter provides the essential tools necessary for employees to define their career direction and move towards it.

When I decided to start my first business, a friend (who was also a leadership coach), interested in my new venture, asked me, 'Why are you doing this?' It was a simple question, but it turned out to be a very powerful one. Although I was excited to explain about my new business, I realised my response was vague and fuzzy and lacked a compelling story to match my passion. This was a game changer for me. After this conversation I locked myself away in my study until I had nutted out my 'why'.

It took me two days to discover that the answer had been there all along, locked away in my core values. It came to me like a blinding flash of light, and it was so simple:

> **At careersmith, we are passionate about careers. We believe every individual has a right to career satisfaction and every organisation has the opportunity to guide and facilitate it. Career satisfaction is a fundamental contributor to individual and organisational success. We are committed to assisting individuals to move towards their career goals and organisations to help them do it.**

This articulated a vision for the business that connected strongly with my core values. It captured the purpose of the business that informed my target market, specific service lines and marketing strategy, and indicators of success that I had previously been struggling to define.

Motivation and determination

Self-efficacy, passion and persistence are three key imperatives for effective goal setting. Goals can change and evolve over time as we mature and develop and as our professional careers move forward. This is quite normal. Mario Andretti, one of the world's most successful racing car drivers, has said, 'Desire is the key to motivation, but it's determination and commitment to an unrelenting pursuit of your goal—a commitment to excellence—that will enable you to attain the success you seek.'

Setting goals is fundamental to driving progress in just about every aspect of human endeavour. Many find goal setting difficult and are held back by procrastination and a sense of inertia, but once they get started they find it doesn't seem as troublesome as they'd expected.

It's all about getting going, making a start, taking the small steps that contribute to bigger successes. In the words of Charlie Chaplin, 'You'll never find a rainbow if you're looking down.'

Some, on the other hand, find they have too many goals and become 'goal diffused'. Research points to goal diffusion as a major derailer of goal achievement. I've found that when I set a clearly defined goal I usually achieve it; conversely when I don't, I rarely move forward.

Knowing where you want to get to is an essential precursor to setting clear goals. In Lewis Carroll's classic book *Alice's Adventures in Wonderland*, Alice encounters the Cheshire Cat sitting on the bough of a tree and asks:

> **'Would you tell me, please, which way I ought to go from here?'**
>
> **'That depends a good deal on where you want to get to,' said the Cat.**
>
> **'I don't much care where—' said Alice.**
>
> **'Then it doesn't matter which way you go,' said the Cat.**
>
> **'—so long as I get SOMEWHERE,' Alice added as an explanation.**

Leaders have a unique opportunity to help their employees set goals and, importantly, to hold their focus on them. The more you can help your employees (and yourself) clearly define career goals, the more likely they will be motivated and successful in moving towards them.

Of course, in the pursuit of our goals, unexpected or chance opportunities will arise. Our ability to recognise and take advantage of opportunities that seem to emerge by sheer chance may cause us to revise, reshape or reprioritise them. I will discuss *planned happenstance theory* in more detail in chapter 10.

Chance does have its place, but what may appear as a chance opportunity can also be a result of the well-laid plans and goals that preceded it. Samuel Goldwyn said, 'The harder I work the luckier I get.'

SMART goal setting

Goal setting is a not an arbitrary activity; it should be a systematic articulation of vision in concrete terms.

SMART provides a simple and robust goal-setting framework. SMART goals are Specific, Measurable, Attractive, Realistic and Time-framed. (They are also a prerequisite of the 'GROW' model used to guide career conversations, and discussed in chapter 10.)

» **Specific:** The better defined and more specific your employees' goals, the more useful they will be to them. Vague, fuzzy goals lead to vague, fuzzy outcomes.

  – *Example:* 'I will complete a postgraduate Diploma of Human Resources part time to achieve a promotion from my current role as Personal Assistant to HR Adviser.'

» **Measurable:** It is essential that our goals are measurable so we can track and evaluate our progress towards them. This allows us to identify and celebrate the key milestones along the way so we know how close we are to achieving our goals and can maintain motivation.

  – *Example:* 'I will study two subjects a semester, with a minimum of a credit pass for each, until I have completed my postgraduate Diploma of Human Resources.'

» **Attractive:** Goals must be attractive for employees to be motivated to pursue them and tackle the inevitable obstacles along the way. This is why it's essential to define your goals carefully and review them regularly to make any adjustments needed. Achieving goals can bring enormous satisfaction and pride.

- *Example:* 'Gaining a postgraduate Diploma of Human Resources will be a critical step towards satisfying and enabling my passion for Human Resources management and give me a great sense of pride.'

» **Realistic:** Our goals must be achievable. It's a waste of precious energy to pursue a goal that is unattainable.

- *Example:* 'I will complete the postgraduate Diploma of Human Resources online as an external student to enable me to study remotely and part time in the evenings and on weekends while continuing to work full time in my current job.'

» **Time-framed:** Setting an achievable time frame holds us accountable to ourselves for our progress. A goal with no time boundaries may never be achieved. As William James said, 'Nothing [is] so fatiguing as the eternal hanging on of an uncompleted task.'

- *Example:* 'I will commence the postgraduate Diploma of Human Resources in the second semester this year and successfully complete it within two years.'

Staying on track

Helping your employees stay on track with their goals is a basic leadership activity. There may be times when they are tempted to give up because they're finding the demands too great. They may just need to recalibrate their goal or modify the time frame. Whatever the case, leaders should provide encouragement and help reduce the employee's feelings of self-doubt or frustration. Winston Churchill advised, 'If you are going through hell, keep going!' I have elaborated on this in relation to understanding the change process in chapter 10.

Anthony Grant offered a simple but very useful model in his book *Solution-Focused Coaching* to help leaders and their employees stay on track once their SMART goals have been established (see figure 6.1).

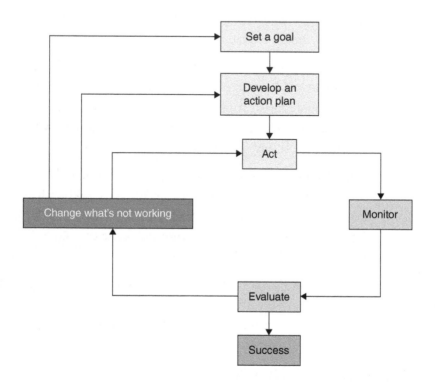

Figure 6.1: Grant's model for staying on track to goal achievement

Source: A. Grant and J. Greene (2003), *Solution-Focused Coaching: Managing People in a Complex World*, Pearson Education.

This model is intuitive and really works! Leaders can help their employees to understand how powerful feedback loops can be in navigating progress and pathways forward. When discussing careers, the model helps to overcome the challenges and setbacks that are an inevitable part of progress.

Tip for leaders

If an employee is finding the work required to achieve their goal overwhelming, help them break it into smaller, more manageable steps. Remind them of the reasons they set the goal in the first place and have them visualise how they will feel when it is achieved. This is a powerful aid to restoring motivation. If it becomes clear that a lack of motivation is more than a temporary setback and that it cannot be revived, then it's time to reassess the goal and, most likely, choose a different one.

Table 6.1 is an example of an action planning chart you could use and recommend for your employees.

Table 6.1: an action planning template

Action	Assigned to	Status	Target date for completion	Date complete
Discuss career goals with manager	Self and manager	Live	July this year	August 20
Complete degree	Self	Live	Nov this year	

Summing up

Leaders can help guide their employees to move through these simple yet powerful goal-monitoring steps. The operative word here is 'guide'. Alison King (1993) coined the expression 'From Sage on the Stage to Guide on the Side' when discussing the role of professors in college classrooms. Her advice holds true for all leaders. It's a privilege to play a role in helping place the stepping stones under your employee's feet.

The employee is the best expert on themselves. Maya Angelou expressed this beautifully when she said, 'If someone shows you who they really are, believe them.' Leaders should adopt an 'ask not tell' approach, using carefully crafted questions to help their employees to arrive at their own destination.

Leaders can play a critical role in ensuring their employees are empowered and liberated by their goals, not constrained or held captive by them. The self-esteem and sense of satisfaction in achieving major career or life goals is hard to match.

Jenny's career story

Jenny came to me as an outplacement client. She was incredibly upset as her company had retrenched her twice within a few weeks from the same job!

Two weeks after her company had first retrenched Jenny they told her they had made a mistake in making her role redundant and rehired her, only to retrench her a second time a month later. Jenny loved her job and had specialised technical skills.

After spending several career coaching sessions with her, largely just listening to help her adjust to the change process, I asked her, 'What do you want to do next?' Jenny explained that she was 'mobile' and had always wanted to work overseas for a 'big brand', and she felt this might be a good time to take that career step. When I challenged Jenny on how serious she was about making this career move, she replied with a resounding, 'Extremely!'

From this landing point I helped Jenny to shape her new career goal, make it SMART and commit it to writing. The goal that emerged had stunning clarity and Jenny's motivation to put it into action grew by the day. Her plan to implement was clear, concise and detailed. It included researching appropriate 'big brand' organisations in Europe that could use her specialised skill set and finding network connections that could help her pull it off.

We worked together on how to manage her personal brand and market her skills and value proposition. This included practising interviews, especially using Skype, with her European counterparts. This took a further couple of months. I helped Jenny to identify potential obstacles, such as around her story on why she had been retrenched, and to develop strategies to overcome them. Jenny worked diligently on her plan, and six months later she landed the perfect role in Belgium for a leading global brand. The hiring company, impressed by her initiative, drive and skills, paid for her relocation to Europe as well as a fully furnished apartment for 12 months while she got settled.

It has been five years since I first sat down with a very emotional and distraught person unsure of her future. Jenny loves her new life and job in Europe. She had successfully turned a serious reverse into a life-changing experience for the better. It took hard work, commitment and courage, but it all started with clearly defining her goals and then actioning them.

Key learnings

When Jenny lost her job through retrenchment, she had an unexpected opportunity to review and reset her career path. Once she had articulated her passion she drafted a written career plan, set SMART goals and systematically executed them for success.

Her story shows the payoff of persistence and resilience and demonstrates how adversity can sometimes open a door to a dream career! Leaders need to keep such possibilities in mind in their career conversations with employees.

Chapter 7
Who motivates the motivator?

'Everyone has been made for some particular work, and the desire for that work has been put in every heart.'
Rumi

The first thing to understand about motivation is that its origins lie deep in our psyche but are also influenced by environmental factors. Motivation is multifaceted and individualistic.

Most leaders know they need to provide a cohesive and inspiring work environment, but is that enough? Much has been said about workplace engagement in recent years, but employers cannot and should not attempt to own an employee's engagement. For one thing, many factors external to the workplace affect employee engagement. As discussed in chapter 1, 'employee experience' is now considered a critical factor that coexists with employee engagement rather than replacing it. That said, the basic building blocks of career satisfaction, motivation and engagement come from the employer providing a workplace culture and physical environment compatible with the values and personal desires of the employees.

Models of human motivation — what works best

There are hundreds of models that attempt to define and explain human motivation, and most have some validity. For our purposes, though, I have highlighted the three that I believe are most useful in the context of career conversations. These are:

1. Abraham Maslow's hierarchy of needs

2. Daniel Pink's theory of intrinsic motivation

3. Max Landsberg's skill/will matrix.

Maslow's hierarchy of needs

First proposed in 1943, Abraham Maslow's hierarchy identified five stages of human needs that culminate in self-actualisation (see figure 7.1).

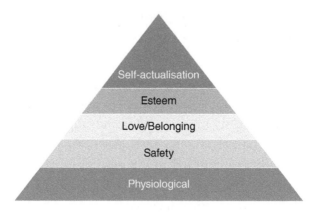

Figure 7.1: Maslow's hierarchy of needs

» **Physiological needs** include food, water, shelter, warmth and sleep.

» **Safety needs** include financial security, personal safety and social stability.

» **Love/belonging needs** include affiliation, friendship, relationships and intimacy.

» **Esteem needs** include self-respect, status, prestige, accomplishment and recognition.

» **Self-actualisation needs** relate to personal growth and achieving one's potential.

According to Maslow, each level of needs, beginning with the basic physiological, must be satisfied before the next level can be achieved. Although conceived many years ago, this model remains relevant to any consideration of motivation, whether in a personal or a career context. For instance, it's hard to be concerned about career development if your employees can't afford to put food on the table or are fearful, overwhelmingly anxious or depressed.

Revisiting Maslow in 2016 in the context of leadership and employee engagement, Shea Heaver mapped the '5 mindsets that individual employees (and by association their teams) can be encouraged to strive for within the workplace'. This inspired me to consider how useful Maslow's model could be for leaders in a career context as well.

For this purpose, in figure 7.2 (overleaf) I have adapted Heaver's concept and diagram to apply Maslow's hierarchy to key career dimensions, along with their enablers.

Let's now look a little closer at each career need and enabler and their relationship to Maslow's model.

Meeting **security needs** (*physiological*) is about having a *fit for purpose* work environment and employment relationships. It's no longer about jobs for life! Leaders need to make sure they are listening and acting decisively in relation to their employees' pain points. One of the key employee criticisms of engagement surveys is that management fails to act on their feedback. In my experience, the only thing worse than not seeking employee

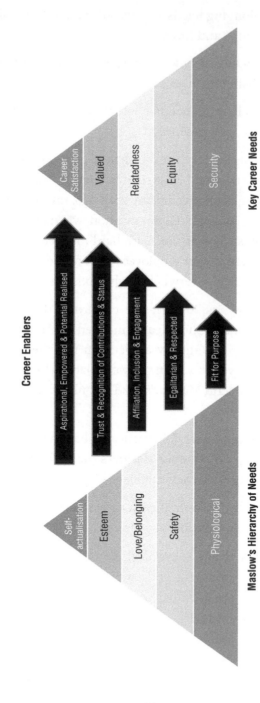

Figure 7.2: a hierarchy of needs for career development (after Maslow)

feedback is failing to deal swiftly with the employee pain points it reveals. This is dynamite for leaders, but paradoxically it's often where you can get big wins from making only small changes to the operating environment.

The security needs level is the base level in the workplace. It's where leaders build trust and confidence in their employees. Career conversations help build these positive and solid foundations. The two operative words for leaders are *listen* and *act*!

Fulfilling **equity needs** (*safety*) is fundamental to the health of employee relationships and relates directly to the quality and scale of their contributions and motivation to innovate. Employees do not perform to their potential, nor are they motivated to innovate, if they feel marginalised and that their input isn't valued or, worse, that their contributions will be mocked. Research shows that employees respond positively to progressive, transparent and open work cultures where they can put forward their views without fear of ridicule in a *safe environment*.

On the flip side, over-controlling managers stifle innovation and discretionary effort by criticising and punishing employees who challenge the status quo — specifically, them! Leaders must be open and ready to recognise and reward employees who demonstrate new ways of thinking and who look outside the square for new ideas in an increasingly dynamic world. Put simply, leaders must create a culture that fosters and nurtures openness and acceptance of new ideas. If we all sit around and just agree with each other, nothing ever happens! A *safe environment* makes it easier for leaders to challenge their employees' career goals when appropriate and in turn relish feedback on their own leadership performance.

Satisfying **relatedness needs** (*love and belonging*) builds on the equity level by developing diversity and collaboration comprehensively throughout the organisation. Achieving unity of purpose while fostering diversity can challenge the most experienced leader. For this reason it's critical for leaders to have a very clear, well-articulated vision of the future, but at the same time to retain flexibility in how their vision can be achieved.

Inclusion is the key to driving simultaneously diverse thought, constructive conflict and productive collaboration. Inclusion is a basic social need; when not reciprocated, it can cause one party to withdraw from the relationship and turn their attention inward towards self and away from colleagues and the organisation. When inclusion is engaged positively—when differing points of view are valued, and openness, respectful communication and acceptance of others are fostered—proactive feedback has the potential to improve work outcomes and practices.

Leaders have a significant role to play in creating and nurturing a culture of inclusion to ensure *all* employees feel they can influence organisational outcomes. Leaders should have the courage to 'take the speed brakes off' their employees and organisation to allow free-flowing innovation and collaboration, confident that such a culture of openness and trust will enhance employee engagement and experience.

Value needs (*esteem*) are a game changer that can lead to organisational functioning of a high order. Building individual and organisational trust is a fundamental leadership responsibility and skill. As discussed in chapter 1, trust is the great enabler of learning and career development. The foundation of effective collaboration is critical to continuous improvement and high performance and is a potent force for self-esteem. Self-esteem is enhanced by a culture of openness in which employees feel valued by their leader and colleagues. Just as self-esteem is closely connected to self-awareness and self-determination, both of which are essential to individual career development (and leadership), leaders who value insight and mutual understanding and develop collaborative organisational systems build highly progressive and successful work cultures.

In my experience, leaders who help employees build their self-esteem see this reflected in their employees' career development and success. This, however, depends on the extent to which employees let you, as their leader, into their world, which in turn depends on the mutual trust in your relationship. This can be kick-started by the leader who is the first to 'open up' and expose their own vulnerabilities. Try it—I'm sure you'll be rewarded!

Career satisfaction needs (*self-actualisation*) sit at the top of the pyramid, the target for all those with achievable life and career goals who seek empowerment, decision autonomy and the prestige of leading and inspiring others. At this level employees strive to better themselves and those around them for the greater good, in the long and short terms, where satisfaction is a tangible outcome. Authentic leaders who are great influencers and coaches thrive at this level by plying their craft with skill and unswerving commitment. These highly capable leaders inspire innovation and drive in their employees and protégés, motivating them to realise their full potential.

Recognising these levels of career needs and their corresponding enablers provides leaders with an opportunity to encourage the behaviours and mindsets required to enhance their leadership effectiveness and build an environment of mutual commitment. Having the opportunity and privilege to help an employee achieve and engage at this level is one of the most rewarding and exhilarating experiences you're likely to have as a leader!

Intrinsic motivation theory

An understanding of intrinsic and extrinsic motivation can provide leaders with valuable insights when in conversation with employees about their careers, or anything else for that matter!

In his book *Drive*, Daniel Pink contrasts intrinsic motivation, which relates to actions and behaviours prompted by the sheer enjoyment the activity brings you, with extrinsic motivation, the focus of which is external reward and punishment mechanisms.

For example, you might pursue a goal that holds a special personal meaning for you or that means your efforts or achievements are recognised by others (intrinsic motivation). Or you might pursue a certain course specifically for its monetary or other tangible reward (extrinsic motivation).

Pink contends that intrinsic motivation outlasts extrinsic motivation and drives superior performance. 'Intrinsically motivated people usually achieve more than their reward-seeking counterparts.' He points out that this does not always apply, though. 'An intense focus on extrinsic rewards can indeed deliver fast results. The trouble is, this approach is difficult to sustain.'

Intrinsic behaviours, Pink suggests, have three key 'nutrients'. These are:

1. **autonomy**—valuing self-determination and engagement over compliance

2. **mastery**—improving professional development and skills to create a sense of achievement and progress

3. **purpose**—pursuing goals that satisfy an intrinsic sense of meaning and purpose (for example, to 'make a difference' rather than just to earn a living).

'According to a raft of studies from SDT [*Self Directed Theory*] researchers,' says Pink, 'people oriented toward autonomy and intrinsic motivation have higher self-esteem, better interpersonal relationships, and greater general well-being than those who are extrinsically motivated.' Pink's view of intrinsic factors as primary drivers of sustained motivation accords with my own experience that as a leader you cannot meaningfully or sustainably motivate anyone, because motivation must come from within your employees rather than external sources.

Tip for leaders

In chapter 1, I discuss career satisfaction as being rooted in one's values. Pink's and Maslow's models both affirm this view, which supports the emphasis I place on this for leaders. Self-determination is critical to an individual's self-efficacy, self-esteem, motivation to succeed and overall progress. However, leaders can provide the environment in which intrinsic factors flourish. This requires that leaders understand where motivators originate and what forces drive them. Unsurprisingly, Pink's three 'nutrients' of intrinsic motivation — autonomy, mastery and purpose — are also essential elements of productive and satisfying career development.

The skill/will matrix — useful ways to lead and coach

Max Landsberg popularised the skill/will matrix in his book *The Tao of Coaching* (1997), drawing on an adaption by Keilty, Goldsmith and Co, Inc. of original work by Paul Hersey and Ken Blanchard. Hersey and Blanchard are best known for their work on situational leadership in the 1970s and 1980s.

This model provides a really useful heuristic to assess the relative contribution of an employee's 'skill' and 'will'. Leaders can use this model as a diagnostic tool for managing, coaching and developing their employees with the objective of moving them towards the High Skill / High Will quadrant (see figure 7.3, overleaf).

The brilliance of this model lies in its simplicity. It is intuitive and in my experience a very reliable leadership and development tool. Following are some leadership tips to manage and develop employees for all four quadrants of the matrix.

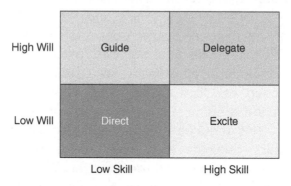

Figure 7.3: the skill/will matrix

Source: M. Landsberg (1997), *The Tao of Coaching*, Knowledge Exchange, LLC, Santa Monica, CA.

DIRECT (LOW SKILL / LOW WILL)

- » Check possible reasons for low 'skill' and 'will'.
- » Identify motivations.
- » Build skill and will.
- » Foster/celebrate small steps and maintain the will.
- » Provide frequent feedback and monitor closely.
- » Train and coach.

GUIDE (LOW SKILL / HIGH WILL)

- » Provide training and coaching.
- » Be responsive to questions and clear with explanations.
- » Foster a fear-free environment that provides opportunities for your employee to take risks and make mistakes to facilitate personal learning and development.
- » Provide feedback.

EXCITE (HIGH SKILL / LOW WILL)

» Check possible reasons for low will.

» Help them to understand what motivates them.

» Encourage a solutions focus (see chapter 9).

» Provide feedback, acknowledge success.

» Monitor your employee.

DELEGATE (HIGH SKILL / HIGH WILL)

» Provide discretion to self-direct and perform.

» Praise and acknowledge success.

» Seek opportunities to further stretch your employee's capabilities (e.g. higher duties).

» Coach and avoid close management.

The skill/will matrix is a great tool for career conversations and development. It can help you shape unique career discussions based on where your employee sits on the matrix at any given time, their progress and what approach might work best for that individual. A subpar performance by a highly capable and experienced employee could be the result of a combination of factors relating to personal, role, employer or career dissatisfaction (high skill / low will).

You can help them uncover their motivations and move forward by asking solution-focused questions, listening intently and encouraging a solution-focused conversation. For example, ask, 'Tell me about a time in your career when you were highly motivated and deliriously happy. What was going on and what were you doing?' Focus on their answer and ask for detail about what made them happy. This might include finding out about anyone who has been instrumental in helping them along the way (and their attributes).

Guiding your employees towards uncovering previously unrecognised patterns and resources that have played a part in their success is a powerful tool for determining what has worked and might help them in the future. This may provide valuable insights into their satisfiers and dissatisfiers and their low will. See chapter 9 for more on the practice and benefits of a solution-focused approach.

Summing up

As a leader, you will find it useful to combine Maslow's needs model, Pink's emphasis on intrinsic motivation and Landsberg's skill/will matrix to form an overall framework to help guide your employees through the motivational drivers of their careers.

This is particularly powerful when combined with the idea of career satisfaction as represented by *motivational*, *career values* and *cultural beliefs* fit discussed in chapter 1. Leaders should also encourage health and wellbeing as a springboard to further career growth and should role model the behaviours they espouse.

In any conversation on work and career development, individual employees must be self-energised and bring their own motivation to the table. They must *want* career satisfaction, not just need it. The reality is, if the employee isn't motivated, there's little a leader can do to help, other than to point out this or that deficiency or perhaps to refer them to an appropriate professional for therapeutic support.

Sonia's career story

Sonia, an events coordinator, was unhappy in her role and shared this with her manager, Jackie, during a routine weekly catch up meeting. Sonia and Jackie had a solid relationship built on mutual trust. Sonia's revelation didn't surprise Jackie, who had noticed how her energy had dropped considerably and quite suddenly in recent weeks. Her efforts to uncover what was wrong, however, failed to shed any light on what had changed for Sonia, either professionally or personally. As the meeting progressed she sensed Sonia's growing frustration. After some deep listening on Jackie's part, and some probing questions, neither felt any closer to understanding what was behind the problem. Jackie decided to conclude the meeting diplomatically and suggested a follow-up meeting the following week (which, by the way, was exactly the right thing to do in the circumstances).

In preparation for the next meeting, Jackie asked Sonia to reflect on which aspects of her role she enjoyed and which she didn't, and to note down if any of those aspects, or the way she had categorised them, had changed over the past year or so. Sonia completed the exercise and brought her notes to their next meeting. The results of this exercise were also inconclusive, though, because they revealed that Sonia enjoyed her role and didn't find the unenjoyable aspects a particular burden, nor did she feel they had changed over the past year.

So Jackie decided to take a different tack (a master stroke): Together, they mapped a timeline of all the events that Sonia felt had affected her significantly over the past year. On the same chart Jackie asked Sonia to rate her energy levels from 1 to 10 during each of these events. A breakthrough!

It turned out that the fall in Sonia's energy corresponded with the company's announcement of its intention to automate various administrative functions. Jackie then asked Sonia what she thought might be going on here. Although not directly affected by the automation, Sonia explained her anxieties that the new technology and restructuring might result in the redundancy of her role too.

Jackie hadn't even considered this possibility and immediately allayed Sonia's fears. What's more, she added, even if her role was affected in the future Sonia had a number of transferable skills that Jackie considered essential to the firm over the long term.

The raising of these issues provided Jackie with an ideal opportunity to help Sonia clarify her career goals and align her development activities to them, and in so doing further strengthen their working relationship.

Key learnings

Jackie's leadership approach was to leverage and further strengthen her trust relationship with Sonia by taking time to unpack and understand the source of Sonia's concerns. Jackie then used this information to help Sonia review and recalibrate her career goals and development. It also reminded Jackie of the importance of not assuming what your employees might be thinking and of opening up an honest dialogue with them in a safe and trusting environment.

Chapter 8
The skilled listener

'I tried to discover, in the rumour of forests and waves, words that other men could not hear, and I pricked up my ears to listen to the revelation of their harmony.'
Gustave Flaubert

If there was just one skill for leaders to master it would be this one—the art of listening! This is an activity in which many leaders have plenty of room for improvement. It's a hugely valuable skill to hone in both our professional and personal lives.

Former US secretary of state Dean Rusk said, 'One of the best ways to persuade others is with your ears—by listening to them.' In his book *What Got You Here Won't Get You There*, Marshall Goldsmith argues that '80 per cent of our success in learning from other people is based upon how well we listen'. Goldsmith also emphasises the importance of not interrupting or finishing the other person's sentences, and resisting any temptation to impress them with how smart or funny you are, and of not being distracted by letting your eyes or attention wander. These are great tips for leaders in any context.

Listening is more than hearing; it's being alert to both verbal and nonverbal cues. The skilled listener is attentive to subtle underlying messages and all that is said and not said, noting the language, tone and posture used in delivery.

The skilled listener also listens to and trusts their intuition. Intuition is not blind faith; more often than not it's a leader's experience talking. Important cues to employee disquiet (or delight) can take many forms. The career story accompanying this chapter highlights how critical employee engagement information can be packaged and communicated in disguise.

Persuade with your ears

We've all heard of disagreements triggered by one party simply hearing something in the other's words different from what was intended. The disagreement is likely to continue until someone breaks the cycle of misunderstanding by first clarifying what has been said and internalised. Sometimes this can take some time! When two people are in a heated argument, have you noticed who's doing the listening? You're right—neither is listening to anything the other person has to say!

This might lead you to ask, 'Why bother arguing at all?' Attentive and insightful listening is an essential skill set for conducting career conversations that are rewarding for both parties. There is no greater respect you can pay someone than to give them your undivided attention and really listen and learn from what they have to say. This helps build rapport, trust and empathy, which are the building blocks of robust relationships.

Sincerity is an imperative leadership trait. The authentic leader demonstrates humility and sincerity in spades. Employees can spot an impostor a mile away and will probably close down or, worse, play their manager at their own game. Both responses are unproductive and a sure-fire way to undermine relationships.

Effective leaders know when and how to use self-disclosure to build connection. This is where self-insight is useful. Self-disclosure is not always appropriate, but it can be a powerful way to demonstrate empathy and humility and to build trust. However, too much or poorly timed self-disclosure can derail relationships, so it should be deployed thoughtfully and prudently.

Four levels of listening

The following four levels of listening (adapted from Julie Starr's 2016 book *The Coaching Manual*, 4th edition) will assist you in focusing your listening skills and provide context for further skills practice and development.

COSMETIC LISTENING

Cosmetic listeners make a show of listening when in fact they're not. This can be a major derailer of career conversations (or any other conversation, for that matter), as it can be perceived as disrespectful.

As a leader, you risk missing critical pertinent information in career conversations, which can lead to wrong conclusions or no conclusions at all! Parties are a common setting for cosmetic listening. Think of a time when the person you were talking to appeared to be preoccupied, their eyes scanning the room as though searching for someone more interesting or important to talk to! Being on the receiving end of such obviously insincere and condescending behaviour can rock your self-esteem and even destroy relationships.

It is vital to show respect and empathy by giving others our full and complete attention. Sometimes even experienced leaders unintentionally slip into cosmetic listening mode. Busy leaders are frequently preoccupied by events outside the career conversation. This lack of focus interferes with their ability to truly listen in a career conversation. Sometimes it might be best to acknowledge the distraction and reschedule the meeting for a later time. Simply apologising and being open and transparent is the best approach in this event.

CONVERSATIONAL LISTENING

Conversational listeners listen superficially, but not to what is actually being said so much as for cues that *they* can now step in and have their say! As with cosmetic listeners, conversational listeners will miss critical information in their self-centred enthusiasm for making their point. When watching two people argue, how often have you been struck by how neither is really listening to the other? Yet argument seems to be as natural as breathing for many of us! Like cosmetic listening, conversational listening undermines career conversations and should be avoided.

ACTIVE LISTENING

Unlike cosmetic and conversational listening, active listening is a valuable skill in career conversations. Active listeners are present and attentive in the here and now. They can accurately record the content of conversations in written notes. Students in a lecture or jurors in a courtroom need to employ active listening. These skills, including the ability to maintain focus in the face of distractions, improve with practice. Being aware of the need to be present and alert, to the extent that you can record or remember the conversation accurately, is a good place to start in getting on the right track.

DEEP LISTENING

Similar to active listening, deep listening requires the listener to be fully in the here and now and acutely aware of what is being said, but it takes this consciousness to the next level. It requires the listener to be *connected* to the speaker and attuned not just to what they are saying but to how they are saying it. Deep listeners are aware of the speaker's tone of voice, body language and level of animation when delivering their messages.

Tips for leaders

The sustained intensity of deep listening over the course of a long conversation can be exhausting, so it's important for leaders to be alert for when they feel the need to break and refresh.

On occasion your employees may choose to share with you more than you would wish about their personal circumstances to add context to the discussion. If this occurs, they need to know two things: firstly, that it's a confidential environment and that you won't share what is discussed with others without their permission (except if they are a danger to themselves or others); and secondly, that if the circumstances require therapy you will refer them to an appropriate professional.

Many organisations have a free Employee Assistance Program (EAP), which may be an appropriate resource for those needing psychological services. If an EAP is not available, encourage them to consult their GP. Either way, it's critical to remember that you are offering a career conversation, not therapy. If in doubt, refer them on rather than being tempted to engage with mental health or social issues that require professional guidance.

As a leader, you will find you can best help your employees when you're in deep listening mode, especially when engaged in career conversations. It clearly demonstrates the care, respect and empathy you have for them. It will help create a safe, fear-free environment in which your employees feel they can be open and frank with you as their leader.

Summing up

This chapter has outlined how critical listening is to communication and how great listeners take a deep approach, using more than their ears, in career conversations.

The best listeners recognise the importance of continuous improvement in developing their listening skills. It's a constant journey of self-discovery on which you should never stop seeking to improve. It's a fundamental key to effective, rewarding and enriching conversations for employees and their leaders. This may sound simple, but it takes practice, and lots of it, to move towards mastery. The positive outcomes make the effort and focus of continuously improving listening skills extremely worthwhile. In my view, there is no more beneficial leadership development to work on!

Zoe's career story

An interstate employee, Zoe, emailed me with a one-sentence question. I was Zoe's two-up leader in the organisational development department of a large company. A talented and technically strong organisational psychologist, Zoe had been with the company for a number of years.

Her personality attributes included an inclination towards introversion, which meant she was not especially comfortable about discussing her attitudes and feelings with others. That said, Zoe was articulate and typically economical with words. You could say she had a no-nonsense and direct communication style, particularly in matters relating to herself.

At first glance, Zoe's question seemed innocuous enough and it would have been really easy to shoot back a simple 'yes'. However, my radar and intuition, combined with my experience in working with Zoe, were setting off a warning bell that encouraged me to probe further. So instead of replying by email, I picked up the phone straight away and called her.

I used direct but open and probing questions to see what reaction I would get.

'Thanks for your email, Zoe,' I said. 'The answer is yes, but I'm curious as to what's behind it.' My gentle probing hit a raw nerve and opened up a long conversation about some things that were troubling Zoe in her local office. It had reached a point where she was seriously considering accepting an unsolicited offer from a competitor. We would have been devastated if Zoe had resigned. Although she felt uncomfortable discussing it, she was evidently relieved to share it with me, even if it was over the phone.

I was able to help settle Zoe's concerns then and there. I followed up with a personal face-to-face visit shortly after to make sure the problem was resolved to her satisfaction. Zoe was delighted with the outcome and remained a loyal high performer.

Key learnings

Good listening is a powerful means of turning a negative employee experience into a positive one. It's one of the easiest and best ways I know of ensuring you engage and retain your talented employees.

Timing and being attuned to your employees' communication styles will strengthen your relationships and sustain their loyalty. Employee issues can often be solved quite painlessly through effective listening and communication.

Trust your intuition and internal radar; don't ignore the signals or procrastinate on taking action, because any delay could mean it will be too late!

Chapter 9
Facilitating communication techniques

'*Mend your speech a little, Lest you may mar your fortunes.*'
William Shakespeare

In chapter 8 I discuss the art of listening and how, when done well, it can be a powerful aid to building trust, demonstrating empathy and establishing a connection with just about anyone. In this chapter, I will expand on this theme by looking at facilitating communication techniques. These include minding your language and choosing your words carefully, applying a growth mindset, reframing for solutions, using mindfulness, and other practical techniques leaders can use to hone their communication skills.

Adopting a growth mindset, assuming positive intent and taking a solutions focus are great places to start.

A growth mindset

American psychologist and researcher Carol Dweck introduced this concept, comparing *fixed mindsets* and *growth mindsets* in her book *Mindset: The New Psychology of Success*. Dweck argues that a growth mindset associates success with effort and attitude and a firm belief in the capacity to learn, grow and develop, whereas a fixed mindset associates failure with a lack of fundamental ability, which is largely innate.

I strongly recommend all leaders to adopt and encourage a growth mindset when holding career conversations. Central to this mindset is a fundamental belief that all individuals, if they choose to, have the opportunity to improve and grow through sustained effort, and that learning supports career growth and development. Effort, Dweck argues in an earlier book, *Self-theories: Their Role in Motivation, Personality, and Development*, 'gives meaning to life'. It means you care about 'something that is important to you', that you 'value things and commit yourself to working toward them'.

This is an outlook of particular importance for those with low levels of self-esteem. It's not positive thinking per se, but rather a belief that career achievement is attributable to our attitude towards success. Believing that success can be achieved with effort, study and application rather than being 'gifted' is crucial to career growth and, ultimately, satisfaction.

In 1993 Anders Ericsson and associates introduced the term *deliberate practice* to describe what's required to achieve mastery in one's field of expertise. Innate talent cannot account for expertise. Science has yet to discover a gene for being a champion golfer, a top musician or an award-winning artist.

What is required is not just any kind of practice or effort, but a very specific type characterised by hard, repetitive work that may not be inherently motivating. Practice should include well-defined and specific goals, meaningful problem-solving feedback, stepping outside our comfort zone, and monitoring our progress towards skill attainment that stretches personal and organisational limits. 'The lack of inherent reward or enjoyment in practice as distinct from the enjoyment of the result (improvement),' Ericsson points out, 'is consistent with the fact that individuals in a domain rarely initiate practice spontaneously.'

Dweck's and Ericsson's research and theories offer leaders important insights into the precursors of success in the short and long term.

Mindfulness

Mindfulness is simple in theory and practice. It means ceasing to do things automatically or unconsciously, but rather living 'in the moment', paying full attention to what you are doing when you are doing it.

We have all eaten a meal while thinking of something else, or perhaps while watching television, and been barely aware of what we are actually eating. So often, preoccupied by the 'noise' of living, we fail to take in all the delights our experiences offer. By slowing down, paying attention, being aware of cultural cues and living in the moment, free of judgement, we can better monitor our reactions and responses to others. Being non-judgemental is critical. Accepting rather than judging what we see and hear helps us to respond more objectively and effectively.

I believe mindfulness is one of the best-kept secrets of the modern leader's toolkit. Developing mindfulness requires meditation training and practice—as little as five minutes a day can be beneficial. You may be surprised by the impact of mindfulness on your wellbeing and how much it can increase your enjoyment of life and work. In my experience, this is a much overlooked imperative for leadership effectiveness.

When I first started practising mindfulness, I kicked off with 10 minutes of meditation a day. I now find 30 minutes is sufficient to set me up to cope effectively with all the challenges of the working day ahead. I find it centres and settles me, particularly when facing a number of competing issues or problems where my thoughts might be racing, my body feeling the effects of stress. Mindfulness can be highly beneficial for your employees' wellbeing too. Being aware in the moment and free of judgement is wonderful for creative and inspiring career conversations!

Tip for leaders

There are many self-help guides to mindfulness meditation. I use the Smiling Minds iPhone app as I always have my phone with me. It means I can meditate wherever and whenever I want, even on the train, so there are no excuses not to! The app is easy to follow and has different levels to accommodate users' varied experience. Best of all, it works! If, as a leader, you are using a meditation training aid such as this one and find it beneficial, then it will give you the confidence (and credibility) to recommend it to your employees.

A solutions focus

Adopting a solutions focus is another powerful tool for driving better and more effective communications. As with a growth mindset, a solutions focus is more than just being 'positive'. It is conceptually simple, but like any other skill it takes practice and will suit leaders who are motivated by working positively and creatively. I first came across the idea in the early noughties and found it such an effective communication tool in all areas of my life that I wished I had discovered it earlier. It even helped me communicate better with my daughters in their teenage years, when nothing else seemed to work!

In their book *The Solutions Focus*, Mark McKergow and Paul Jackson stress that the key to finding solutions is to keep things simple and to deliberately focus on solutions, not problems. The authors provide excellent tips on how to develop a solutions focus and demonstrate the rewards this approach brings. Here I outline some of the authors' ideas and tips. I also share some examples adapted from Anthony Grant's applications, which I have found especially helpful for getting the most out of a solutions focus and putting it into practice in career conversations.

In my experience, when leaders focus on problems, the problems seem to grow larger— until they create feelings of overwhelming frustration, which lead to inertia, inaction and a sense of being 'stuck'. Have you ever been in a meeting where participants discuss a problem over and over and are mentally exhausted when the solution fails to appear? Focusing on problems may not be helpful in finding the solutions. Most often a fresh approach is called for. The way we talk about problems can give them oxygen. We're more likely to make progress if we change the way we talk about them by reframing our conversations in favour of solutions talk. This requires thinking differently about 'problems' by viewing them not as obstacles but as ways forward for which we have yet to determine the right solution!

There will be times when we must start by focusing on a problem but then get quickly back to solutions talk and actions. Both leaders and employees are best served by directing their energy to challenges to which they can ascribe a solution. This might seem obvious, but I have seen too many individuals and teams commit time, energy and resources to unsolvable problems.

If a problem is described in vague terms it's almost certain to be unsolvable. My advice is when you hit an unsolvable problem, assign it elsewhere and move on!

A solutions focus is more about tracking progress than diagnosing problems. This in itself is more inspiring and motivating than describing problems in detail, which can simply dull the senses rather than enlightening us. As Jackson and McKergow point out, the solutions focus practitioner keeps things simple by making a study of what people are doing when things are 'better'.

Further, looking for exceptions, when things are or were better, is a key lever. Exceptions often hold the key, as they may point to all or part of the solution, though it may be disguised and need teasing out. I have found this a really powerful tool, particularly when clients seem to be *stuck* in the problem.

REFRAMING PROBLEM-FOCUSED LANGUAGE

Here are some examples of how leaders can reframe problem-focused career questions they may be tempted to ask their employees by using more helpful, solution-focused language.

Problem-focused question:
'You seem dissatisfied with your career, what do you think the problem is?'

Reframed as a solution-focused question:
'Can you point to a time when you were happy in your work or broader career?'

Follow-up questions:
'What was going on? Can you tell me more about that?'

Problem-focused question:
'You don't seem to get along with your peers—do you know where you're going wrong?'

Reframed as a solution-focused question:
'So you want to get along with your peers? [This is a somewhat rhetorical question used to reinforce a more positive mindset.] Can you tell me about an example of where and when you have got on well with one of your peers?'

Follow-up questions:
'Can you tell me more about that?' or

'What could be a small step you could take to do things differently?' or

'Can you tell me about a time when you did this successfully?"

Problem-focused question:
'Why have you taken such a long time to address your career issues?'

Reframed as a solution-focused question:
'You've really stuck it out in your career, through thick and thin—how have managed to cope and do this so well?'

Follow-up questions:
'Who has been helpful to your career so far, and what did they do to assist you?' or

'Who else might be able to help?'

These examples demonstrate how powerful simple reframing can be in moving a problem-focused conversation onto a more productive and useful solution path.

Encouraging solution talk provides the context and environment for more helpful career conversations with employees, particularly if they feel 'stuck'. Shifting our language from a problem focus to a solution focus can be subtle and takes conscious practice, but mastering this skill is thoroughly worth the effort. Collaborating with our employees to co-construct career solutions is a powerful, empowering and immersive experience that helps drive highly productive connections.

Achieving mastery takes a great deal of practice. That said, you can start using this communication technique straight away, taking small, incremental steps towards becoming a skilled practitioner. Immediate results provide the best motivation to keep practising. Remember, as Jackson and McKergow argue, to keep it simple, make a start, and if you find something that works then keep doing it.

Tips for leaders

Leaders can encourage solution talk by being interested and attentive when employees use solution language; they can discourage problem talk by being less receptive when employees use problem-focused language. As Jackson and McKergow advise, focus on highlighting strengths and resources, and explaining progress. Look for good and better (not right and wrong), and pay attention to what people are doing when things are better. Remember to be on the lookout for employees' getting stuck on unsolvable problems.

While a solutions focus is a powerful communication tool that has the potential to move your employees to productive solutions quickly, leaders should be careful not to rush their employees to solutions too quickly, before they're ready to consider what's next or get into the frame of mind for change. This is a judgement call, but a really important one. If you're concerned that one of your employees might not be ready, don't be afraid to slow the process down.

Additional useful communication techniques

I encourage leaders to follow former PepsiCo CEO Indra Nooyi's advice and 'assume positive intent' in all discussions, and I don't do this lightly. It may not be easy if your employee is being flat-out unreasonable, but trust me, the principle is always worth remembering and applying in all your interactions with others, as it will set a positive, non-judgemental tone for the conversation.

Here are some further communication tips to help you guide career conversations:

» Be open in your approach, explaining the reasons behind the information you share or the questions you ask. For example:

  – 'John, I'd like to share some background on current career pathways because it may help guide your career aspirations. Is that okay?'

» Ask permission to offer advice or support. Unsolicited advice can breed resentment! For example:

  – 'John, I have a suggestion that might help. Would you like me to share it with you?'

» Respond empathetically with a view to enhancing their self-esteem. Think about how you might feel in their position. Look for ways to convey your understanding and sensitivity to their feelings and position.

» Use self-disclosure, if appropriate. For example:

  – 'John, I understand how much this concerns you. I've been there myself, and this is how I approached it ...'

» Acknowledge emotions and avoid judgement (refer to Marion's career story in chapter 3) to help calm employees who are stressed or upset. This can help reduce tensions and redirect the conversation onto a more meaningful (solution-focused) path. For example:

   – 'John, I can see how much this has upset you. Would you like me to help?'

Tip for leaders

I recommend you to take time out to read Founder and Principal of Incorporate Psychology Matthew Dale's article titled 'Improving Your Communication and Social Skills', which provides further, very useful tips on enhancing your communication skills. Check the References and further reading section of this book for source details.

Summing up

As leaders, our effectiveness in helping our employees to navigate their career development depends very much on our perspective, or how we choose look at things. Look at this picture. Do you see a young woman or an old crone? Or does your mind's eye flick backwards and forwards between each perspective?

This exercise illustrates how easy it is to see the same thing in quite different ways, sometimes at the same time! When considering what an employee shows us through the lens of their life and career, what we 'see' passes through our own filters of experience and psychology.

We can help facilitate better outcomes by mindfully paying attention to our language, attitudes and communication styles. Remember, the solutions to any problems are likely to exist already, even if in disguise; we just need to recognise and build on them.

When it's so easy to choose techniques that support growth and produce positive outcomes, why would any leader choose to do otherwise?

Peter's career story

One day Peter, an aspiring young junior salesman who had joined the sales team less than a year before, knocked on my office door and asked if I had a minute. I was the sales manager of a large industrial products firm.

The minute turned into a two-hour career discussion. Peter shared with me a problem that was causing him significant anxiety and even loss of sleep. Peter was convinced that one of his co-workers, Anthony, was 'white-anting' him, undermining his career prospects. In sharing this, Peter's posture and language were uncharacteristically aggressive.

To help build empathy and take some of the charge out of Peter's emotions, I acknowledged that I could see he was upset and understood how he might feel. When I asked him what his evidence was for feeling this way, his answers were vague, such as, 'Oh, I heard on the grapevine that Anthony wasn't helping my cause'.

Over time this led Peter to conclude that Anthony was actively and deliberately trying to subvert his standing in the company by unjustly criticising his performance. Peter had concluded that Anthony was jealous of his achievements and saw him as a threat to his own career progression. He also made it clear that he didn't like Anthony and therefore hadn't reached out to him over the matter.

It was true that, in this sales-focused company, a competitive spirit was encouraged, not just between members of the sales team, but throughout the organisation. For the most part, competition between employees had a positive influence on the organisation, in which openness, trust and constructive conflict were encouraged and role modelled by the leadership team. Listening to Peter's tone and language, I suspected there was more to unpack here.

After some careful probing, Peter was still unable to point to any clear evidence to support his assertions. At this point I felt it was time to steer the conversation away from the 'problem' of Anthony's alleged behaviour. I reframed Peter's expressed feelings about Anthony by asking him, 'So you want to get along with Anthony?' Peter replied, 'Of course I do.' Which completely changed the tenor and direction of the conversation.

Had Peter replied in the negative, this would have uncovered a quite different issue to be resolved! In solutions focus mode, I went looking for exceptions: I asked Peter to tell me about a time or times when he had got along with Anthony. This enabled him to take a more circumspect and rational view of his relationship with Anthony by highlighting occasions when Anthony had actively helped him gain new leads and contacts that directly led to sales wins. That is, times when the relationship was already working positively! As the discussion progressed, Peter began to realise that what he was being told by others about what Anthony was saying about him flew in the face of his own experience of working with Anthony.

The obvious question was why Anthony would want to hold him back after helping him succeed? It just didn't stack up. At that point I asked Peter what he thought was going on. Peter canvassed a few options but after reflecting, and in the light of no hard evidence, he concluded that this perceived issue was a complete misunderstanding driven by throwaway comments passed through a number of parties and taken out of context.

Shifting the discussion towards thinking of his relationship with Anthony not as a problem but as part of the solution had the desired effect by fostering a more constructive and useful approach and outlook.

Peter realised that he had misread Anthony's motives and that his career could actually continue to benefit from Anthony's help.

Peter decided to proactively reach out to him to nurture the relationship. Applying a growth mindset and solution-focused approach, together we explored other development initiatives that Peter could realistically pursue with Anthony.

Although Peter's relationship with Anthony had prompted the discussion, it turned out that Peter's perception of his own capability and development was really at the heart of his concerns, and not his perceived problem with Anthony. Having identified this as the central issue I could not only help Peter gain a more productive view of his relationship with Anthony but also set some SMART development goals that he could start working on straight way. This helped Peter move forward from a negative, anxious mindset to feeling motivated and re-energised. Peter's 'have you got a minute?' question turned into a two-hour career conversation that was inspiring for both of us!

Key learnings

In this career story the presenting 'problem' of Peter's relationship with Anthony turned out to be a red herring. Resolving their relationship issue would not in itself have got Peter closer to his development goals. It took a fresh approach, careful listening, reframing and empathy, combined with a fundamental belief in a growth mindset, to 'unpack' the issue and move the conversation to a more useful place. The moment when your employee gets that 'light bulb' insight is very powerful and exciting. Sometimes you won't know when it will come, just that it will!

Leaders need to take the necessary time and mindful care with their employees to allow these processes to unfold. Such an investment will pay off in the long run, especially for leaders who are inclined to pretend the issues don't exist or will somehow miraculously solve themselves without help.

Chapter 10
Structuring unstructured conversations

'Conversation. What is it? A mystery! It's the art of never seeming bored, of touching everything with interest, of pleasing with trifles, of being fascinating with nothing at all.'
Guy de Maupassant

It might seem paradoxical but there is a structure to having unstructured career conversations. In my experience of coaching leaders, or directly coaching employees in my various roles as a leader, I have found a narrative approach to career conversations to be one of the most effective ways of highlighting patterns and themes and potential pathways forward in career work. It may appear to employees as a 'freewheeling' conversation. What sits behind this approach, however, is a structure that informs the language, shape and direction of what is discussed and how the emerging information is used. In the context of career conversations, a narrative approach should guide an employee to tell their story by following a chronological sequence of events.

The narrative approach

The narrative approach is particularly effective as it has the potential to unlock in the minds of employees suppressed or forgotten events or achievements they have experienced over the course of their career and life. They could be aware of an event but not regard it as an achievement—a tenure milestone, for example, or an instance when they helped a colleague to succeed.

Helping your employees tell their story assists them in constructing a timeline of the events and milestones that have shaped their career, from leaving school to the present day. It also helps for them to identify individuals—a colleague, previous manager, friend or family member, or even groups of people such as clubs or teams—who may have influenced their decisions or contributed to their career development or advancement in the past.

A narrative approach can be boiled down to helping employees recognise key transition points. It's important, and consistent with the solution-focused principles outlined in chapter 9, to identify and analyse the drivers and contextual influences that have supported previous successful transitions and to use these skills and this knowledge to facilitate future transitions. This can assist in identifying patterns and themes that could again be useful in planning and navigating their future careers. It's a simple but powerful tool for leaders to guide enlightening career conversations with their employees, and you will be amazed at the results when you start applying it. That said, as with all tools it takes practice to master!

Planned happenstance

Unplanned career events, unexpected opportunities and just plain luck can all play a role in our career development and success. Most could point to a bit of luck that helped them along their career journey. John Krumboltz, Kathleen Mitchell and Al Levin devised a career theory called *planned happenstance* (referred to in chapters 5 and 6). Essentially, they suggest that opportunities can emerge quite unexpectedly when actively doing 'the right kinds of things'—for example, being prepared and developing one's skills to capitalise on any chance events that may pop up from time to time and to convert them into career opportunities.

In a 1999 paper, Krumboltz and associates identify five key skills that individuals should develop (and leaders can help them do this) in order to generate and make the most of chance events, and to recognise them as career opportunities. These are:

1. **Curiosity**—provides inspiration to help drive the search for learning opportunities. This is fundamental to proactive career development for both leaders and their employees.

2. **Persistence**—means persevering and putting in the effort despite facing obstacles, challenges and setbacks. So many people give up too soon, just as they are about to make a breakthrough, or they leave a company because of a bad boss, only to find the boss leaves the organisation soon after.

3. **Flexibility**—remaining open-minded and agile in our thinking and attitude to changing circumstances, and therefore viewing change as an opportunity for career development. Flexibility is so valuable to leadership and career development.

4. **Optimism**—possessing self-efficacy and seeing new opportunities everywhere. This means having a solutions focus and a positive disposition and outlook, while viewing problems as challenges to act on and resolve.

5. **Risk-taking**—avoiding procrastination, being decisive and taking action even if you're unsure of what might happen. This means not letting fear of failure or the unknown stop you from seeking out and acting on new career opportunities.

In a 2009 paper Krumboltz writes, 'The Happenstance Learning Theory explains that the career destiny of each individual cannot be predicted in advance but is a function of countless planned and unplanned learning experiences beginning at birth.' Leaders can (and should) add to their employees' learning experiences by encouraging them to be proactive in their career development and be acutely attuned to recognise and act on opportunities that arise.

My own career has benefited from many unplanned events. That said, looking back, I can identify times when I prepared myself, both consciously and unconsciously, to take advantage of these opportunities. I have reinvented myself several times over my career. After leaving secondary school I embarked on a science degree, planned from school because I had an aptitude for it. I disliked it intensely and as a result dropped out of first-year studies. I then entered the business world in the paper industry (unplanned and secured by chance as there happened to be a job opening at the right time). I quickly found I loved both the industry and the business world, particularly sales and marketing.

I went on to study marketing and spent more than 20 years rising through the organisational ranks. I enjoyed several chief executive roles, culminating in my appointment to one of the biggest roles at that time in the Australian paper merchanting industry. Over that period, I took advantage of many opportunities that presented (some planned, some not), but I can point to many occasions on which I very deliberately and purposefully set myself up for success. I also benefited from the great help of a number of very supportive managers, coaches, mentors, colleagues and friends.

In the course of various leadership roles in the paper industry, I became fascinated by human behaviour, career development and leadership theory and practice. This fascination turned out to be stronger than that I held for the paper industry, so I decided to explore a career change. At this stage in my career, I decided I wanted to help many organisations and not just the one I was working for. After researching a number of options, I moved into a highly regarded human resource consulting firm that had all the service lines (and more) that I was interested in.

I spent more than 10 years consulting to a wide range of public- and private-sector clients with a variety of consulting firms and also held a number of senior leadership roles. The verdict was in: I loved consulting! This experience inspired me to co-found and lead my own HR consultancy, specialising in—you guessed it—career and leadership development and HR recruitment.

So I can attest to the fact that planned happenstance theory has played a very real and profound role in my life and career, most often in an extremely positive way! Doing the 'right things' doesn't guarantee success, though I (along with my clients) have found it definitely helps! All leaders have the opportunity to help their employees do the same.

The key is to keep an open mind, expect the unexpected, recognise when these unplanned events arise, treat them as a gift and take advantage of them by taking appropriate action.

In the introduction of this book, I called out the need for leaders to be agile in their approach to how, when and where they engage their employees in career conversations. Common sense tells us that these conversations should be held in a confidential environment, free of distractions, but in practice this is not always so easy to manage in today's world of open-plan offices and fast-paced, dynamic workplaces. Sometimes leaders just need to grab the 'moment' as it arises. This is a good example of acting on or using planned happenstance theory. Putting off a career discussion to a later date could very well mean it ends up being too late to save an employment relationship. Seize the moment in this scenario!

As a leader you will most likely diarise regular career discussions, but sometimes great career conversations result from unplanned, in-the-moment meetings. I want to emphasise that while scheduled career development meetings work well, so too do career conversations done 'on the fly'. As a leader, you just need to recognise these opportunities and make time for them when needed. This is easier said than done, but an imperative nonetheless. Putting off a career conversation can be perilous to employee engagement and retention. You need to exercise judgement on what can wait and what can't. This is a fundamental and crucial leadership capability that, from my experience, remains in short supply!

Change and transition in careers

Transitions and change are not always linear and are not always easy to create and sustain, yet change is nearly always a necessary ingredient in career growth and development. Making and dealing with change can feel difficult and even daunting. As discussed in chapter 2, after working with many individuals (and groups) going through significant change, I have come to understand that people do not fear change but rather fear *being changed*.

Advocating change therefore may well be required in some career conversations. This is a crucial skill in itself because leaders can play a critical role in leading, advocating and managing change for both individuals and their organisations.

When thinking about change and how to inspire and encourage it, leaders can apply a number of useful models, some of which are outlined here.

BRIDGES' MODEL OF TRANSITION

For change consultant William Bridges, transition is about starting something new, which implies letting something go. I have adapted Bridges' transition model in figure 10.1, which points to a neutral zone between *letting go* and *starting something new* to explain how important these phases are to career transition and development. The *neutral zone* can be thought of as an 'ambivalence phase' that can be frustrating for employees (and their leaders!) but is an important one to move through. In my experience, we can be at our most creative in times of uncertainty, so ambivalence is not a bad thing. It can be quite useful and is certainly normal.

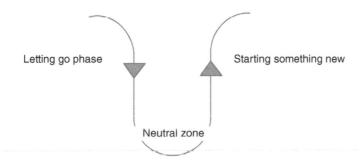

Figure 10.1: Bridges' transition model

Adapted from W. Bridges and S. Bridges (2017), *Managing Transitions: Making the Most of Change* (rev. 4th edn), Hodder & Stoughton, London.

Paradoxically, leaders have an opportunity to help their employees embrace uncertainty and ambiguity as a pathway to clarity. A feeling of complete exasperation from not seeing a way forward can trigger a breakthrough, when we discover exactly what to do! This is when leaders can play a vital role in helping their employees, particularly if they feel stuck in their career, to move forward towards starting something new.

Tip for leaders

Helping your employees move from the 'letting go', neutral or ambivalence phase can be trickier than you think. Moving them from one phase to another takes great care, skill and patience.

While the objective is to help them migrate to the right of the curve towards starting something new, leaders should also apply a steadying hand so employees don't rush forward before they're ready. They need to assimilate their transition to accepting a new reality (just as they did when absorbing new solutions as discussed in chapter 9).

GRANT'S 'HOUSE OF CHANGE' MODEL

Anthony Grant believes that to sustain real and lasting change in our lives we need to change our thoughts, feelings and behaviour, which interact with our situation to bring about change and enable goal achievement (see figure 10.2).

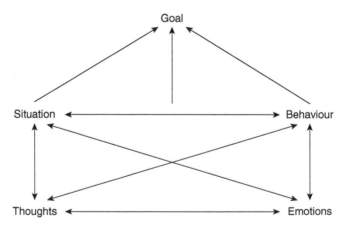

Figure 10.2: Grant's 'House of Change' model

Source: J. Greene & A. Grant (2003), *Solution-Focused Coaching*, Pearson Education, UK.

Grant points out that if the foundations of the house aren't firm, then the whole structure including the roof (the goal) are at risk. More to the point, changing only one or two of the pillars won't facilitate the change we may be seeking. For example, if we change the way we think about something but fail to change our behaviour, then we jeopardise the necessary change. If we change our *situation* without changing how we think, feel and behave, then making and sustaining the change required to achieve our goal becomes highly unlikely.

Grant's model asserts that we need to redesign all four pillars of the house to effect and sustain the change required to reach our goal. This concept is particularly useful for leaders seeking to help employees who may be able to set goals but who struggle to maintain their focus on them. Leaders can observe this in an employee who experiences frequent, short-lived forays in their career progress or multiple employers over a relatively short time period. Applying the 'House of Change' concept in these circumstances, leaders can help their employees to examine and, if necessary, redesign their house.

A MODEL OF INTENTIONAL CHANGE

The process of change, whether in yourself or in others, can seem complicated, challenging and far from easy to achieve and sustain. I'd love a dollar for every time I've been asked by an exasperated leader, 'Why did they do that?' when talking about an employee's 'inexplicable' behaviour.

Change is a very well researched topic, yet many leaders are still bewildered by how to lead and manage it. The problem isn't change itself, so much as how people think about it. By that I mean many leaders have a tendency to overcomplicate it. This can be seen when people set goals that require moving mountains then get frustrated and even give up when the goal remains elusive. Who can blame them? For example, having just taken on an entry-level leadership role for the first time, they immediately set their sights on progressing to a senior management position within 12 months. Such an aspiration is unrealistic and is bound to lead to frustration and disappointment. Here is where leaders can help their employees recalibrate their goals, as discussed in chapter 6.

Change experts today generally accept that effective change involves several key stages. James Prochaska, John Norcross and Carlo DiClemente developed their Transtheoretical Model to conceptually articulate the process of intentional behaviour change that focuses on the decision-making pathways and can be applied to almost any area of an individual's life. Figure 10.3, adapted from their model, depicts change behaviour as a continuing loop of actions that begins when we first start thinking about making a change (*contemplation*).

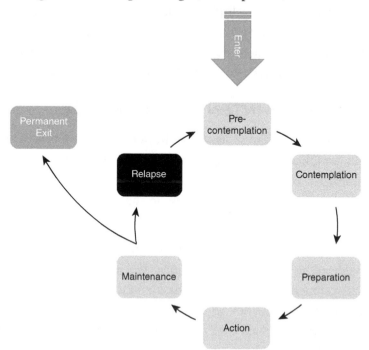

Figure 10.3: a model of intentional change

Pre-contemplation denotes the time before we consider making a change. Once we have thought about making a change (*contemplation*), we start preparing to make the necessary adjustments (*preparation*) and taking deliberate steps (*action*) towards change behaviour. From there we enter the *maintenance* stage, during which we need only a low-energy approach to prevent a relapse. Better still, we exit the loop having successfully made and sustained the change we wanted, which has now become a permanent part of our personality. As this model highlights, *relapse* is a normal part of the behaviour change process.

It's rare that change is a linear progression uninterrupted by setbacks. For example, it's not unusual for smokers to experience numerous relapses when trying to quit smoking. In fact, the framework of this model has been used in a number of studies in relation to smoking cessation. In recent times Australian anti-smoking campaigns have featured television advertising that stresses that relapse is normal and encourages those trying to quit to keep trying.

As an example of the model's application in a career scenario, a performance review holds a surprise and to avoid holding back potential career advancement we are asked to change our professional behaviour in some way (*pre-contemplation*, since we weren't aware of the need to change). The boss provides compelling behavioural examples of why this is necessary; we accept the feedback and start to think about what needs to happen (*contemplation*), and we engage a coach to help make the change (*preparation*).

We work positively with our coach and proactively seek feedback on our progress (*action*). Having successfully changed our behaviour, we incorporate this into our work style (*maintenance*, and exit the process). Perhaps after making good progress we temporarily slip back into our old ways (*relapse*). We *contemplate* re-engaging the behaviour change process so the change loop continues.

Failing is great for success!

Failing nurtures courage and helps build resilience. It is surely one of the best ways of learning. Indeed, I believe that failure should be a compulsory subject in every business school or university.

Committed to the benefits of failure, *The New York Times* reported that Smith College in Northampton, Massachusetts, added failure to the syllabus in 2017. Rachel Simmons, a leadership development specialist at Smith, remarks, 'What we're trying to teach is that failure is not a bug of learning, it's the feature.'

The initiative, called 'Failing Well', is aimed at destigmatising failure and teaching students how to cope with and learn from disappointments and setbacks. The program includes workshops on impostor syndrome along with discussions on perfectionism and fostering resilience. Those who fall prey to impostor syndrome are convinced they are 'frauds' and undeserving of success and recognition, despite evidence to the contrary. Instead, they attribute to luck or good timing their ability to deceive others into thinking they are more capable or intelligent than they really are.

Perfectionism, while driving success, can also hold individuals back. For example, if leaders project their exacting high standards onto their protégés, this can potentially interfere with their employees' own development and confidence, particularly if, in the leader's eyes, they don't 'measure up'. Rachel Tyson, psychologist with Incorporate Psychology, has written an excellent article on imposter syndrome that I encourage you to read (see References and further reading at the back of this book).

Smith College encourages students to take healthy risks (and feel comfortable doing so), to explore new disciplines and to try new experiences. Students who complete the program receive a *Certificate of Failure*, which declares that it's possible to 'screw up, bomb or otherwise fail at one or more relationships … and still be a totally worthy, utterly excellent human'.

In a career context, it's important for leaders to recognise that not every career conversation will 'make a difference' but every conversation will contribute to progress, even if this is not apparent at the time. Progress, no matter how small, matters and is valuable. Baby steps are just as important as giant leaps; indeed, they are often more useful to making and measuring progress.

This is where leaders will find a good dose of humility—and, at appropriate times, self-disclosure of their own failures—very useful. By showing employees how disappointments, failures and setbacks contributed to their career success, they can role model their intrinsic benefits to overall career development. This can help build confidence in their protégés, allowing them to feel more comfortable in making their own mistakes. As is clearly highlighted in Prochaska, Norcross and DiClemente's model, by stumbling and reflecting we are set up to make navigational changes and limit the recurrence of unwanted experiences.

The key is to be empowered, not imprisoned, by our mistakes. When our mind is in a state of confusion, we can be at our most creative! The way forward might already exist but be disguised. Sometimes we just need to take a leap of faith and see what happens! Leaders can play a powerful part in helping their employees break free of the confines of convention, stereotypes and norms, and their own usual thinking patterns, and cut a new path forward.

The GROW model — a useful tool for structuring effective career conversations

The GROW model provides a sensible, easy-to-follow and effective framework for narrative-style career conversations in which the leaders collaboratively co-construct the way forward with their employee.

The original authorship of this model is unclear, though Sir John Whitmore, Alex Fine and Graham Alexander all made significant contributions to its development. Max Landsberg also described it and its applications in coaching in his book *The Tao of Coaching*.

The GROW model is broken down into four elements.

GOALS

Setting SMART goals (see chapter 6).

For leaders this might be as simple as asking, 'What would you like to achieve or leave with at the conclusion of this meeting?'

REALITY

The leader checks the employee's current reality by exploring what's really going on and comparing this with what they might wish to be happening. This may include asking what's stopping them achieving their goals and whether they would like to modify their goals or choose a new one. The leader might simply ask, 'What's happened since we last met?' or 'What has happened in the past week or two?'

OPTIONS

The leader helps their employee to identify and consider possible options. It's empowering to have options; conversely, it's disempowering to feel no options exist! Collaborative brainstorming is a helpful activity here. The leader may ask, for example, 'What do you see as realistic options?' or 'What else could you do?' or 'What has worked in the past and what do you see as the next step?' These questions are designed to put the power in the hands of the employee to help them move forward positively, creatively and practically.

WRAP-UP

This is where leader and employee plan the next steps. It will usually involve considering obstacles to achieving the goals and concrete strategies to overcome them. This commonly takes the form of action planning with specific, clearly assigned, goal-oriented actions with target dates for completion.

Tip for leaders

'RE-GROW', described by Grant (2003), adapts the GROW model that may be used for successive career conversations, where the 'RE' refers to Review and Evaluate. Here the employee, in collaboration with their leader, reviews and evaluates actions, successes and outcomes towards goals attainment, then follows the GROW framework.

Figures 10.4 and 10.5 (overleaf) illustrate simple GROW and RE-GROW templates.

Goal(s)
Remember to make them *SMART*.
Ask: *'What would you like to achieve?'*

Reality
Checks the current reality and goals.
Ask: *'What's happened since we last met?'*

Options
Brainstorm realistic options and stay solution focused.
Ask: *'What's worked in the past?'*

Wrap-up
Plan the next steps. Consider possible obstacles and how to overcome them.
Ask: *'What specific steps will you take next and when?'*

Figure 10.4: the GROW template

Source: Adapted from A. Grant and J. Greene (2003), *Solution-Focused Coaching*, Pearson Education, UK.

Review and Evaluate

... actions, successes and outcomes towards goals attainment. Remember to stay solution focused.

Ask: *'What progress have you made towards your goals since we last met?'*

Goal(s)

Remember to make them *SMART*.

Ask: *'What would you like to achieve?'*

Reality

Check the current reality and goals.

Ask: *'What's happened since we last met?'*

Options

Brainstorm realistic options, remembering to stay solution focused.

Ask: *'What has worked in the past?'*

Wrap-up

Plan the next steps. Consider possible obstacles and how to overcome them?

Ask: *'What specific steps will you take next and when?'*

Figure 10.5: the RE-GROW template

Source: Adapted from A. Grant and J. Greene (2003), *Solution-Focused Coaching*, Pearson Education, UK.

Tips for leaders

Making notes is a good way to keep track of your conversation. Make sure you ask permission to take notes and let your employee know what you'll do with them to protect their privacy, and tell them they can review them at any time.

A useful technique to add emphasis to a point or an idea is to place your pen or pencil with the tip pointing towards the word or idea that you want to focus on. This is a powerful yet unobtrusive way to maintain attention on key ideas. Try it!

Summing up

This chapter has reviewed some basic concepts and approaches to conducting unstructured conversations to benefit and inform the language, shape and direction of career discussions. A narrative approach to career conversations is recommended for exploring career patterns, themes and potential pathways forward. The experience of failing has been demonstrated to be surprisingly helpful to career development. Leaders need to be on the lookout for the negative influence of impostor syndrome and perfectionism on employees' self-image and performance. Unplanned events also play an important role in career development, and both leaders and employees need to make the most of unexpected opportunities.

This chapter looked at several useful models that can help leaders understand the change process and its application to careers. The GROW templates are a great tool to keep employees focused on making progress and to achieve productive outcomes from every career conversation.

Ben's career story

Ben is a technical expert in his field. Based on his success, he was moved from research and development into sales and very soon after, in mid career, was promoted to sales management. Ben hadn't applied for a job since his employer hired him in their graduate intake, more than 20 years ago. He took advantage of career opportunities as they presented and his career flourished, but now he was struggling to find meaning in his work. His passion for his work had dipped and he found he lacked motivation and energy, as was evident to his peers.

Ben approached Human Resources for help. A recent 360-degree feedback survey indicated that his subordinates had also noticed a drop in Ben's passion and energy. His work performance, along with sales revenue, had shown a drop over the last three quarters. Human Resources were sympathetic. They suspected that sales management wasn't a good fit for Ben and probed further for possible reasons for this. Ben's HR business partner encouraged him to have a career conversation with his manager, Adam.

Ben wasn't overly enthusiastic and avoided this conversation for some time, until finally Adam called Ben into his office and asked him straight out what was wrong. Adam referred to Ben's recent 360-degree survey feedback, flagging sales performance and noticeable lack of energy. Ben acknowledged he was struggling in his role as sales manager and didn't know why he lacked the motivation to fix things. Adam was frustrated with Ben but needed to find a solution to the falling sales revenues fast. He told Ben, using quite direct language, to 'sort himself out and pull his socks up or he'd be replaced'.

Ben left this discussion upset and was at a complete loss to know what to do next. He returned to Human Resources to report the outcome but was told there was little more they could do to help. They urged him to try to work things out with Adam.

Ben saw that neither Adam nor HR were going to be useful to him, so he sought the help of a professional career coach. The coach used a narrative approach in working with him and had him complete the career drivers exercise. Taking a structured approach of debriefing his career driver results combined with the narrative-style conversations helped Ben to unpack his current situation, rediscover his career motivators and demotivators, and refocus on his passion, technical expertise.

It became apparent that no-one in Ben's company had asked if he wanted to be sales manager; rather, they just expected him to jump at it because it meant a promotion and more money. Ben had been flattered by the confidence they showed in him and, although he felt uncertain about it, accepted the role. Ben's career coach helped him to uncover that his technical expertise was his number one career driver. The lack of opportunity for this career driver in his sales management role was a major source of his discontent, which helped explain his lack of motivation and corresponding performance deficit.

A few weeks later, having regained his career focus and clarity, Ben returned to Adam and requested a transfer back to research and development. Adam was relieved by Ben's decision, which offered the bonus of allowing the company to retain a high-performing and talented employee.

Ben was amazed by how a structured approach to his career discussions and career development had, in a relatively short space of time, allowed him to explore and refine his true passion.

Key learnings

While Ben and his company both came out winners, there were multiple failure points along the way. These began with Ben's promotion into a role without a robust selection process and were compounded by the organisation's failure to provide career support when the error was first suspected. Those failures were exacerbated when Ben's boss threatened him with dismissal and Human Resources offered little follow-up support.

Although Ben eventually found success, he could have been saved from an unhappy period in his career, and the company could have avoided the revenue losses resulting from his subpar performance, if Ben's manager and/or Human Resources had used some of the career tools discussed in this book.

Chapter 11

Leading a career conversation

'To be able to ask a question clearly is two-thirds of the way to getting it answered.'
John Ruskin

You are now ready to lead a career conversation, but it's worth reminding yourself that it is a *conversation*! Satisfying conversations require both parties to truly listen to each other and to respond respectfully and empathetically. As with most skills, practice makes perfect. Having a genuine sense of curiosity and interest in your employee, and a mental library of thought-starting questions to call on, is a great starting point for a positive career discussion.

Always adopt an 'ask, not tell' approach to career coaching conversations. Crafting the right questions is essential for productive career discussions. Open, probing, thought-provoking questions will encourage useful self-reflection in your employees. As discussed in chapter 8, finely tuned listening skills are essential for effective career conversations. Listening closely in the here and now will lead you towards appropriate follow-up questions.

Here are a few sample questions to help kick-start your career conversation with your employee:

- » Why do you stay? / What might lure you away? / What would keep you here?

- » What were you promised when you were recruited, and did it turn out as you expected?

- » What do you find is the most energising aspect of your work?

- » What makes you feel like taking a day off?

- » What do you like about your job? / Are your career drivers and aspirations being satisfied?

- » What don't you enjoy about your job?

- » What did you like about your prior job? / What kept you there?

- » Are you being challenged/recognised/trained/given feedback enough?

- » What would make things better here for you?

- » What do you want to be doing three years from now?

In my experience, leaders can find some of these questions challenging and difficult to ask. Some feel uncomfortable asking questions that might elicit a negative response or worry about starting a conversation they'd rather not have! Yet asking the challenging questions that inspire employees to find their own solutions is exactly what leaders should be doing. It's a key capability that all effective leaders should develop and hone.

Tips for leaders

A word on the value of silence. Paradoxically, silence used well is one of the most powerful tools in your career conversations toolkit. Many of us find silence during a conversation awkward and uncomfortable and often can't resist the urge to fill the void with talk. My advice to leaders is *don't*! Sometimes it's best to let the silence just hang and to wait for the other party to respond, no matter how uncomfortable it feels. Filling in the gaps can sidetrack the conversation, stifle your employee's reflection time and unintentionally subvert useful conversation points. When you feel the urge to break the silence, just *zip the lip*!

If the silence persists unproductively, you might ask them, for example, 'What's running through your mind right now?' An open-ended question of this kind can be a gentle, non-confrontational way to move the conversation forward.

Asking the right questions means doing your homework, having a 'loose' game plan and thought-out options before entering into a career discussion, but being prepared to change course if necessary. The emphasis here is on *options*. It's important not to rehearse a conversation, because you have no idea where it might go. Think about the questions you might ask, but don't stick rigidly to a plan if it clearly needs to be abandoned when the conversation takes an unexpected direction. The risk here is of completely missing the mark with your employee, and of both of you walking away feeling disconnected, demotivated and dissatisfied. This can make any follow-up career discussion with your employee more difficult.

If your employee does surprise you, it's critical that you are conversationally agile enough to change your original plan in order to hold their interest and truly connect with them. Turning up to a career meeting with fixed ideas about what you believe is best for your employee says more about your needs than about what your employee actually needs or wants. Your employee is the expert on themselves, or should be, so let them be the expert. That said, just like all experts, employees need non-judgemental help and guidance, and to be challenged from time to time!

Summing up

Effective career conversations start with asking the right questions. Knowing the right questions to ask can be tricky, but following the simple advice in this chapter will get you started and help you hone your skills in this area.

The careful use of silence can be surprisingly productive, particularly when your employee is uncertain what they think or how to express their response to one of your questions.

Leaders should prepare thoroughly before a one-on-one with their employee. Thinking carefully about how they might best approach the meeting, and the kinds of questions that might be most constructive, will provide a great foundation for a successful career conversation.

Patricia's career story

Knowing my passion for career development, a colleague invited me to a presentation given by Patricia, a highly educated management consultant, about her career journey.

Patricia delivered her career story in an amusing and entertaining style. She presented as a confident, articulate speaker and clearly enjoyed taking to the stage to share her career story. She described herself as having more degrees than a thermometer! She spoke candidly about the ups and downs and metaphorical 'blind alleys' she experienced before, in her mid forties, finding what she referred to as her dream career as an educator in the field of commerce.

Patricia painted her story as perfectly illustrating the value of persistence, of not being afraid to try out a variety of career paths, until you land on the one that provides career satisfaction. At the end of the presentation, my colleague leaned over to me and asked what I thought of the presentation. I responded, 'It was very entertaining.' When probed further, I replied, after a pause, 'I don't buy it.' My colleague, who knew me well, asked, 'What do you mean?' I replied, 'While it was certainly an entertaining speech, and delivered with great conviction, it left me feeling that something was missing.' It caused me to question whether Patricia had indeed found her dream career.

Back in my office I reflected on my response but still couldn't quite put my finger on the reason I felt this way. I was curious to explore further why this lingering doubt remained.

My colleague knew Patricia quite well too and, knowing how I felt, asked if I would be open to meeting with her. A few weeks later I met with Patricia over a coffee. Patricia opened the conversation by asking what I had thought of her presentation. I responded as candidly as I had before. Patricia fell silent and stared down at her coffee, playing with the pattern the barista had created on surface for what seemed like an eternity.

The silence was excruciating. I could see my response had touched a raw nerve. I knew intuitively, though, that no matter how awkward it felt, it was crucial to let the silence hang. In reality, it could only have lasted a minute or two but it felt like forever! Patricia finally looked up from her coffee and, looking me straight in the eye, asked, 'How did you know?'

Those four words led us into a rich career discussion that unearthed valuable self-insights for Patricia around why she felt stuck. During the conversation Patricia confronted the reality of what had been holding her back from career satisfaction and her real 'dream career'.

While it transpired that several issues were at play, the central one was that she had been consumed with pleasing others (including her parents) and doing what they thought she should do rather than what she truly wanted for herself. I have struck this career derailer many times in my coaching experience.

Over the rest of the coffee meeting, we brainstormed, canvassing options to overcome the obstacles she perceived as preventing her from finding true career satisfaction.

At the end of our meeting Patricia admitted she had found the discussion a cathartic experience. She shared that she had never discussed much of what we spoke of that day and that she felt like a huge burden had been lifted from her shoulders.

Key learnings

This career story demonstrates the value of techniques discussed in this and previous chapters for leading effective career conversations, including:

» carefully constructed, open-ended questions

» deliberate silence

» empathy

» considered probing and listening in the here and now.

In this case, an informal, 90-minute meeting over coffee led to a potentially life- and career-changing outcome!

Chapter 12
Ethics and protocols for career development

'In matters of conscience, the law of the majority has no place.'
Mahatma Gandhi

In chapter 1 I discuss the importance of building and nurturing trust to effective career conversations and indeed to leadership. This chapter outlines some of the key ethical principles and protocols for leaders aiming to build and maintain this trust and to create a safe and respectful environment for employees.

Ethics play a critical role in every aspect of organisational life, but never more so than when discussing, guiding and nurturing the individual careers of those you lead. While ethical considerations provide a blueprint for appropriate behaviour, no list can be exhaustive enough to cover all possible scenarios or eventualities.

In my experience, sometimes there is no one rule or clear answer to an ethical dilemma. Wise judgement is needed to produce the best outcome. Recognising that such a dilemma exists is the critical prerequisite to dealing effectively and appropriately with it. Ethics are grounded in values. Whenever I have struggled to find the best way forward, I have gone back to my values and more often than not found my answer there!

Tips for leaders

Here are some useful tips for ethical decision making:

1. Recognise that ethical dilemmas exist.

2. Know where an ethical dilemma has arisen.

3. Identify the relevant ethical issues.

4. Analyse and assess the short- and long-term risks and benefits associated with alternate courses of action.

5. Select a solution or solutions, and critically evaluate the potential outcomes of each one.

6. Reflect on the experience and share non-confidential aspects with colleagues.

7. Learn and grow professionally from addressing the ethical dilemma or situation.

8. Apply what you have learned to future situations.

Confidentiality is critical

Respecting confidentiality is critical. Employees need to be sure that their leader will create a safe environment for them, and this includes treating any information shared as confidential. This does not mean leaders should be plundering their dark secrets—quite the contrary—but employees need to be confident that they can discuss anything they feel will help their career without their being judged and any confidences being shared with others without their approval.

Leaders may at times be tempted to seek resolution by discussing what has been shared with others in the organisation. This temptation must be resisted at all costs, except in the unlikely event that it might involve self-harm or harm to others, in which case the appropriate professional should be informed immediately. If you feel it would be helpful to share with a third party anything that your employee has told you, check for alignment and seek the employee's express approval before doing so. Then, and only then, can this be done.

A cautionary word on therapy

Leaders should be cautious not to stray into or practise any form of therapy. If you suspect your employee is suffering from depression, or some other mental, physical or social condition, then refer them to the firm's Employee Assistance Program (EAP), if you have one, or to the relevant health professional, as discussed in chapter 8. You may need to actively encourage your employee to take this step, but you should then leave it to them to act on your advice. Knowing how and when to do this is often a source of anxiety for leaders. Unfortunately, there's no rule book to follow here. Only be sure not to engage in anything that even approximates therapy!

Logistics

Leaders should always keep the logistics in mind, including the physical environment where they hold career conversations. Following are some key do's and don'ts:

1. **Don't** sit behind your desk if the discussion is held in your office; come around the other side so you can be on the same level as your employee.

2. **Don't** hold the meetings in 'fish bowl' style office or meeting room, where the exchange is fully visible to others in the office. A fish bowl meeting may embarrass your employee, stifle any plain speaking or distract from your career conversation.

3. **Do** have water and tissues ready in case they're needed.

4. **Do** switch off phones or turn them to silent, and make sure the meeting is not disturbed, other than in an emergency.

5. **Do** set a defined time frame for the career discussion. An hour to an hour and a half is optimal in my experience.

6. **Do** avoid rescheduling career discussion meetings. Constant rescheduling sends the message to your employee that these sessions are not important to you as their leader.

7. **Do** avoid scheduling other meetings immediately before or after, in case your discussion needs longer than anticipated. Sometimes breaking off the discussion at the wrong point can be counterproductive, leaving your employee hanging and unnecessarily anxious.

8. Do take notes, but ask permission from your employee to do so. Let them know your purpose in taking notes, and that they will be safely stored and can be viewed by them at any time.

Summing up

Ethics and appropriate protocols matter! As a leader, it's your responsibility to role model the behaviours you expect from others, to 'walk the talk'! Here are some useful techniques and ethical considerations when holding career conversations:

» Use an 'ask, not tell' approach. Resist the temptation to slip into instructional mode; instead, think of the best question to guide your employee to their own conclusions.

» Encourage your employee to research options they are interested in, to seek a mentor and to develop their own internal and external networks.

» Don't breach confidentially, unless self-harm or harm to others is a concern.

» Avoid judgement.

» Be alert to discrimination of all kinds.

Laura and Lisa's career story

Laura, a senior project manager and team leader of a major technical systems upgrade project for a large company, found herself in a tricky ethical leadership dilemma. Lisa, a key project team member with highly specialised and hard-to-find technical knowledge and a close personal friend of Laura's, was going through a difficult time in her private life.

Lisa was facing the convergence of several personal challenges. While she tried to keep her personal challenges from her colleagues, and in particular from her friend and boss Laura, her situation had reached a crisis point, and she was finding it increasingly difficult to hide the negative impacts on her work performance from the team.

Laura and her colleagues noticed that Lisa's work quality was dropping off and she was missing key project deadlines and milestones. The other team members felt that Laura was covering for Lisa because they were friends, and they weren't happy about it. While they were concerned for Lisa's wellbeing, they were also annoyed with her for potentially undermining their individual performances and the project's overall success.

Laura became very worried for Lisa, both as her friend and as her manager. Lisa had not shared any of her troubling personal circumstances with Laura or anyone else at work. This also concerned Laura, who was mystified and a little hurt that Lisa hadn't confided in her about what was going on. But she chose to respect Lisa's privacy and to wait for her to share it with her when she was ready.

Finally, after coming under pressure from every direction, Laura decided she could wait no longer to confront Lisa. Laura scheduled a meeting with Lisa for later that morning. In the meeting Lisa opened up and confidentially told her story.

Lisa felt bad about her own circumstances but also bad about the impact this had on the project and on Laura personally. So she told her all about her personal troubles, which were a combination of health and partnership issues. As Lisa's story unfolded Laura was shocked by her revelations and concerned for her wellbeing. Using solution-focused language, she asked Lisa how she had found the resilience to keep going and generally coping so well in the circumstances. Lisa found strength in Laura's empathy and felt as though a load had been lifted off her shoulders already simply from sharing her story with her.

Laura could see what this interaction would mean for Lisa's work on the project and instinctively knew what the next steps should be. She offered Lisa the services of the company's Employee Assistance Program (EAP) and encouraged her to use it, which Lisa assured her she would do straight away. Laura also offered her extended leave with full pay so she could concentrate on dealing with her private issues. Moreover, she promised to hold Lisa's job for her until she returned. Lisa jumped at the offer.

Having suspected that something of the kind might be at play, Laura had already been quietly 'feeling out' a former colleague with similar technical skills to Lisa on taking up a contract role to fill in for Lisa until her return.

The great news was the contract offer was accepted. Finally things were starting to fall into place, and for the first time in weeks Laura felt that the project would soon be back on track.

Her dilemma now, though, was what she could tell the project steering committee, her team and the HR director about the changes and actions taken without breaching Lisa's confidentiality. Laura thought long and hard about this. Others would demand an explanation for what had happened, yet she knew that she couldn't under any circumstances compromise Lisa's confidentiality. With Lisa's permission, Laura decided to be transparent about what Lisa would be doing moving forward, without misrepresenting Lisa's predicament but without sharing any of the confidential aspects. This was critical not only to Lisa but also to Laura's colleagues.

The outcome was that Lisa engaged with the company's EAP service, which she found extremely helpful, and took six weeks off work to recover and resolve her personal issues. The contractor who stepped into Lisa's role did an excellent job, so much so that Laura extended his contract to assist Lisa after she returned to help her settle back in.

Laura took some time out to reflect on all that had happened. She felt happy about some aspects of the process and wondered what she could have done better. She was satisfied with her handling of the ethical issues but came to the conclusion that she might have found a way to intervene earlier in the process. She also thought she might have shared the responsibility by asking for help from her manager or HR without comprising Lisa's confidentiality, rather than taking all the weight on her own shoulders.

With her problems now mostly sorted, Lisa returned to work refreshed and with a renewed enthusiasm for the job she loved, and her work performance was back to her usual exemplary standard. Her return was welcomed and celebrated by the project team, especially Laura! The project was now back on track and hitting all its milestones, and the team was powering through the work as never before.

Laura's careful and thoughtful handling of the ethical issues had a welcome and surprisingly beneficial impact on the project, the team, Laura's leadership standing in the company and her professional development, along with her friendship with Lisa.

Key learnings

Sometimes ethical or other issues turn out to be not as hard to deal with when we apply basic principles of ethical behaviour (mainly confidentiality in this career story) in our leadership approach.

Ethical issues present in many shades of grey, which means it's not always easy to see the right course of action to take. My advice is to draw on your values for guidance, seek input from trusted advisers where this doesn't compromise confidentiality or other ethical considerations, and carefully consider your timing. In following your values, don't be afraid to stand alone in your decisions and actions.

It's not always easy to get the timing right when dealing with ethical issues. Jumping in too soon can be just as bad as procrastinating. In my experience, leaving issues to fester can be really problematic. In the end, leaders must exercise their best judgement and follow their instincts.

It can be very easy to rush to judgement when you don't know all the facts of a matter. Things may not always be what they seem. Leaders can't always share confidential information for ethical reasons, yet this discretion can reflect poorly on them. It's also critical to let your values guide you on when you need to stand firm. In my experience this leadership approach is nearly always recognised, respected and rewarded in time. Leaders must consider how, when and where they act.

(continued)

Key learnings *(cont'd)*

If you feel that sharing any part of your employee's story might benefit them and/or the organisation, then always discuss this with them and seek their permission.

Reflect, reflect and reflect some more. Afterwards take some time, as Laura did, to consider what went well and also what might have been done better.

Chapter 13

Now you're ready to hold career conversations!

'*The secret of getting ahead is getting started.*'
Mark Twain

Congratulations! Now, with all the learnings of the preceding chapters under your belt, you're ready to hold effective and meaningful career conversations with your employees. Let's take stock of some of the career coaching techniques outlined in this book to help consolidate your learning. Then the only thing left to do is to embed these ideas through practice!

A review of learnings

In chapter 1 I argued the rationale for the provision of organisational career development support by leaders. I discussed the changing world of work, including the emerging gig economy.

The *career leadership levers model* outlined the key strategies available to leaders to help facilitate and implement their employees' career options and decisions. To assist you in assimilating your learning, I'll briefly summarise how each set of career levers connects to the advice, tools and recommendations provided throughout the book.

SELF-INSIGHT AND GOAL SETTING

In chapters 2, 3, 4 and 6, I discussed the importance of developing self-insight, including the role of emotional intelligence, and how this can be used for setting corresponding career goals and vision that align with your employees' hopes and dreams, skills and values.

MOTIVATION AND STRESS CONTROL

Chapter 7 explored the importance of intrinsic motivation. Sharing this knowledge with employees helps them understand their own motivational drivers and the need to maintain emotional and stress control for career success, particularly in the face of challenges and obstacles.

DEEP LISTENING AND CONNECTIVITY

Chapters 8 and 9 outlined how leaders can connect effectively to build trust, empathy and rapport, and to identify career themes and patterns. By helping employees determine what has (and hasn't) worked for them in the past, leaders can move them towards their career goals and vision, and towards making wise career decisions.

REFRAMING THINKING AND COMMUNICATIONS

Chapters 8, 9, 10 and 11 looked at some great communication tools. I discussed how leaders can use the GROW model to structure career conversations and the importance of asking your employees questions that challenge their conventional, sometimes entrenched thinking. Unstructured conversations play a valuable role in helping employees recognise and act on chance opportunities. Reframing for a growth mindset and solution-focused questions are especially valuable techniques for helping leaders challenge employees to overcome obstacles and build confidence (even when they are not so sure) by looking at things differently.

PERSONAL BRANDING, TRANSFERABLE SKILLS AND ETHICS

Chapters 2, 5, 10, 11 and 12 offered tips on how to use personal branding to advance your career, and the essential messages and techniques for leaders to share with their employees. We explored why and how transferable skills and continuous learning are more important than ever, and unpacked ethical principles and protocols in relation to career conversations, and why they matter.

The written career plan

A written career plan is essential (see table 13.1, overleaf, for a template for this). Remember, it's not a career plan unless it's written down! This is where the rubber hits the road. Here's where you bring all your learnings from this book into play in order to encourage your employees to develop their own plan. They may need your help, though.

If appropriate, consider showing them your own career plan and sharing any challenges you had in completing and executing it. This will demonstrate openness and humility that may help to reduce any uncertainties or anxieties they may have in planning their career. It can also shed light on any lingering issues your employees may not yet have disclosed.

Table 13.1: sample career plan template

Name:	Date:
Step 1. Career review Include: – key roles, milestones and achievements – study and qualifications – the top three roles that have brought you most satisfaction. Note if all your values were represented in these roles. Who have been your role models or have influenced your career decisions? How have they done this?	
Your notes	
Step 2. Self-evaluation List your: – career drivers – attributes – career values – skills you want to use – passions and interests – personal SWOT.	
Your notes	

Step 3. Career options
- Develop and research options.
  Assess and evaluate options.

Your notes

Step 4. Career vision and goals
- Write a few sentences that describe your career vision.
- Identify three career goals to support your vision. (Don't have too many and remember to make them SMART.)
- Review goals every six months and adjust as necessary.

Your notes

Career goal #1

Career goal #2

Career goal #3

(continued)

Table 13.1: sample career plan template *(cont'd)*

Step 5. Self-marketing
– What is your brand statement? (If it could talk, what would it say?)
– Update your résumé targeted to career goals.
– Keep social media (LinkedIn) up to date.
– Organise evidence of qualifications.
– Make sure referees are current.
– Implement strategic network plan.
– Practise interview skills.
Your notes
Step 6. Professional development
– Research and identify formal and informal training programs aligned to achievement of your career goals.
– Seek out a mentor/coach.
– Look for suitable role models to study and learn from.
– Research professional memberships to support your career.
– Commit to reading blogs, books and articles in and beyond your career interests for a minimum of two hours per week.
Your notes

Step 7. Action planning

Prepare a detailed action plan that lists all critical activities, who will be involved, and dates for completion that support and are aligned to your career goals.

Your notes

Step 8. Review

Review successes, goals, self-marketing and overall plan every six months.

Your notes

Tips for readers

When it comes to career plans, try not to let your employees spend too much time overthinking things or wordsmithing; instead, focus them on action and just getting it written down using the template. The only people who will read it are the employee concerned and you, as their leader.

Wrapping up

All the tools you need are here. I hope this book gives you as a leader the confidence to inspire and manage creative and meaningful career conversations with your employees. What's essential is plenty of practice to help you embed the skills you've learned.

Don't be afraid to experiment and add your own personal touches and try new ways to engage your employees in their careers through deliberate conversations. A mentor to help guide you will always be valuable.

Maintaining your learning in this field of leadership practice will ensure you best serve your employees and your company. In my view, this is paramount to attracting and retaining talented employees in a world of work that's changing and evolving at a rate and on a scale we have never seen before.

Finally, remember that everyone wins when career conversations are done well. Good luck with yours!

References and further reading

Angus, C. (2015). Future Workforce Trends in NSW: Emerging technologies and their potential impact. Briefing Paper No. 13/2015. NSW Parliamentary Research Service.

Bennett, J. (2017). 'On Campus, Failure Is on the Syllabus'. *New York Times*, June 24.

Bridges, W. & Bridges, S. (2017). *Managing Transitions: Making the most of change* (rev. 4th edn). Hodder & Stoughton, London.

Brown, D. & Brooks, L. (1990). *Career Choice and Development: Applying contemporary theories to practice* (2nd edn), Jossey-Bass, USA.

Caminiti, S. (2018). 'The Dream Job That's All the Rage across America', CNBC.com.

Carroll, L. (1865). *Alice's Adventures in Wonderland*. Macmillan, London.

Clance, P.R. (2013). 'Imposter Phenomenon (IP)'. http://paulineroseclance.com.

Clutterbuck, D. & Megginson, D. (1999). *Mentoring Executives & Directors*. Butterworth Heinemann, Oxford, UK.

Dale, M. (2018). 'Improving Your Communication & Social Skills'. Incorporate Psychology, ICP Human Solutions blog, March 23.

Doran, G. (1981). 'There's a S.M.A.R.T way to write management's goals and objectives', PDF, pp 35–6, AMA Forum.

Dudley, G. & Goodson, L. (2009). *The Psychology of Sales Call Reluctance*. Behavioral Sciences Press, Dallas, TX.

Dweck, C. (2007). 'Self-theories: Their role in motivation, personality, and development', *Essays in Social Psychology* (1st edn). Psychology Press, London.

Dweck, C. (2007). *Mindset: The New Psychology of Success*. Ballantine Books, USA.

Dweck, C. (2017). *Mindset: Changing the way you think to fulfil your potential*. Robinson Publishing, UK.

Ericsson, A. & Pool, R. (2017). *Peak Secrets from the New Science of Expertise*. Eamon Dolan/Mariner Books.

Ericsson, A., Krampe, R. & Tesch-Romer, C. (1993). 'The Role of Deliberate Practice in the Acquisition of Expert Performance', *Psychological Review*, 100(3), 363–406. American Psychological Association.

Francis, D. (1985). *Managing Your Own Career*, pp. 45–72. Collins, London.

Freeman, S.C. (1993). 'Donald Super: A perspective on career development' (1991 Interview), *Journal of Career Development*, 19(4). Human Sciences Press, USA.

Gallup (2017). State of the American Workplace.

Gelard, D. & Gelard, K. (2001). *Basic Personal Counselling.* Pearson Education, Frenchs Forest, NSW.

Gladwell, M. (2000). *The Tipping Point.* Little, Brown and Company, Boston, MA.

Global Workplace Analytics & Flexjobs (2017). State of Telecommuting in the U.S. Employee Workforce.

Goldsmith, M. & Reiter, M. (2007). *What Got You Here Won't Get You There.* Hyperion, New York.

Goleman, D., Boyatzis, R. & McKee, A. (2002). *The New Leaders.* Time Warner, UK.

Goleman, D., Boyatzis, R. & McKee, A. (2013). *Primal Leadership: Unleashing the power of emotional intelligence.* Harvard Business Review Press, Boston, MA.

Grant, A. & Greene, J. (2001). *Coach Yourself.* Pearson Education, Harlow, London.

Grant, A. & Greene, J. (2003). *Solution-Focused Coaching: Managing people in a complex world.* Pearson Education Limited, UK.

Heaver, S. (2016). 'Maslow in the Context of Leadership and Employee Engagement'. Business 2 Community, USA.

Hersey, P. & Blanchard, K.H. (1988). *Management of Organisational Behaviour* (5th edn), pp. 169–201. Prentice Hall, Englewood Cliffs, NJ.

Jackson, P. & McKergow, M. (2007). *The Solutions Focus.* Nicholas Brealey International, London, UK.

Kabat-Zinn, J. (1994) *Wherever You Go, There You Are.* Hyperion, New York.

Kaye, M., Annesley, M. & Shultz, K. (2016). *Retirement: The psychology of reinvention*. Darling Kindersley, London.

King, A. (1993). 'From Sage on the Stage to Guide on the Side'. *College Teaching*, 41(1), Winter, pp. 30–5. Taylor & Francis.

Krumboltz, J. (2009). 'The Happenstance Learning Theory'. *Journal of Career Assessment*, 17, 135. Sage Publications.

Krumboltz, J. Leven, L. & Mitchell, K. (1999). 'Planned Happenstance: Constructing unexpected career opportunities', *Journal of Counseling and Development*, vol. 77, Spring.

Landsberg, M. (1997). *The Tao of Coaching*. Knowledge Exchange, LLC, Santa Monica, CA.

Lencioni, P. (2012). *The Advantage*. Jossey-Bass, San Francisco, CA.

LinkedIn Communications Team (2017). 'Eighty-percent of professionals consider networking important to career success'. LinkedIn 2017 global survey results article.

Michaels, E., Handfield-Jones, H. & Axelrod, B. (2001). *The War for Talent*. Harvard Business School Press, Boston, MA.

Morgan, J. (2017). *The Employee Experience Advantage*. Wiley, New Jersey, USA.

Morgan, J. (2017). 'What's the Difference Between Employee Engagement and Experience?' *Inc.*, July 28.

Newman, M. (2007). *Emotional Capitalists*. Wiley, Brisbane.

Noer, D.M. (1993). *Healing the Wounds: Overcoming the trauma of layoffs and revitalizing downsized organisations*. Jossey-Bass, San Francisco.

Noer, D.M. (1997). *Breaking Free: A prescription for personal and organizational change*. Jossey-Bass, San Francisco.

Nooyi, I. 'The best advice I ever got' (interview), *Fortune* magazine, April 30.

Orem, D. (2018). 'On My Mind: Teaching failure might actually be a good thing'. National Association of Independent Schools.

Pfeffer, J (1998). *The Human Equation*. Harvard Business School Press, Boston, MA.

Phillips, B. (2018). 'Automation Report: Regional Australia to be hit hardest'. Adzuna blog, March 21.

Pink, D. (2009). *Drive: The surprising truth about what motivates us*. Riverhead Books, USA.

Prochaska, J. & DiClemente, C. (1994). *The Transtheoretical Approach*. Krieger, Florida, USA.

Rousseau, D.M. (1989). 'Psychological and Implied Contracts in Organizations'. *Employee Responsibilities and Rights Journal*, 2(2).

Rousseau, D. M. (1995). *Psychological Contracts in Organizations: Understanding written and unwritten agreements*. Sage Publications, USA.

Salomone, P.R. (1996). 'Tracing Super's Theory of Vocational Development: A 40-year retrospective'. *Journal of Career Development*, 22(3), Spring, 2996. Human Sciences Press.

Sharf, R. (2002). *Applying Career Development Theory to Counselling*. Wadsworth Group, USA.

Sinclair, A. (2007). *Leadership for the Disillusioned*. Allen & Unwin, Crows Nest, NSW.

Starr, J. (2016). *The Coaching Manual: The definitive guide to the process, principles and skills of personal coaching* (4th edn). Pearson.

Sternberg, R.J., Grigorenko, E. & Jarvin, L. (2015). *Teaching for Wisdom, Intelligence, Creativity, and Success*. Skyhorse Publishing, New York.

Super, D.E. (1957). *The Psychology of Careers*. Joanna Cotler Books, USA.

Tay, R. (2013). *Career Conversations: 20 professionals share the secrets of their success.* Marshall Cavendish International (Asia).

Tyson, R. (2017). 'Tackling Imposter Syndrome'. Incorporate Psychology. ICP Human Solutions blog, January 31.

Whitmore, J. (1992). *Coaching for Performance.* Nicholas Brealey, London.

Whitworth, L., Kim-House, H. & Sandal, P. (1998). *Co-active Coaching.* Davies-Black Publishing, Palo Alto, CA.

Index

risk-taking 126, 135
role modelling 2, 31, 68, 120, 135

satisfaction, career 9–11, 39, 42, 87, 93; *see also* engagement; motivation
—competence and 9–10
—definitions 10
—values and 95
self-actualisation *see* Maslow's hierarchy of needs
self-awareness 28, 29–30, 33, 37; *see also* self-insight, career
—building 25–36
—career drivers 25–26
—career story 34–36
—coaching 29–30
—coaching competencies 30–32
—emotional intelligence 27–28
—intelligence, varieties of 28–29
—leadership tips 28
—values 25–26
self-determination 95
self-disclosure 103, 135
self-efficacy 78, 95, 125
self-esteem 72, 92–93, 94, 95, 103, 110, 117
self-insight, career 12, 13, 37–63, 103, 164
—attributes 39, 40
—attributes exercise 40, 62
—career change story 61–63
—driver descriptors 51
—drivers 39, 42–51
—drivers exercise 42–48, 62
—drivers profiles 49–51
—exercises 40–41, 43–48, 62
—leadership tips 43, 57
—letter from the future 59–60
—reviewing own career 25–36, 37–63
—skills, identifying 51–56, 62
—SWOT analysis, personal 57–59

—transferable skills 39, 51–56, 62
—values 39–41
—values exercise 41, 62
self-knowledge 25–36
self-management 28
self-reflection 18–19
self-respect 89
sincerity 6, 102, 103
skills, transferable 18, 21–22, 39, 62, 51–56, 72–75, 100, 165
skill/will matrix, Landsberg's 88
social awareness 28, 29–30
social media 65–66, 67–68
solutions focus 97, 109, 112–116, 120–122, 165
stages, career 2–3, 5, 6
stress control 12, 13, 164
succession planning 1
SWOT analysis, personal 57–59

technology and work 15, 16
telecommuting 16
tipping point 66
tips for leaders *see* leadership tips
transferable skills *see* skills, transferable
trust 2, 13, 28,30, 91, 92–93, 99, 100, 102, 103, 108, 109, 120, 153, 164

values 11, 25–26, 39–41, 78, 87
—defined 39
—exercise 41, 62
vision 12–13, 24
—defined 77

war for talent 21
work, changing nature of 15–17
—effect on careers 17–18
work environment 87, 89–92, 95